BEETHOVEN

Symphonie Nr. 9 in d-moll

Symphony No. 9 in D minor

op. 125

D1930407

Herausgegeben von / Edited by
Jonathan Del Mar

Bärenreiter Kassel · Basel · London · New York · Prag
TP 909

INHALT / CONTENTS

SYMPHONIE NR. 9 / SYMPHONY NO. 9

BESETZUNG

Kleine Flöte, 2 Flöten, 2 Oboen,
2 Klarinetten, 2 Fagotte, Kontrafagott;
4 Hörner, 2 Trompeten, 3 Posaunen;
Pauken, Schlagwerk; Streicher;
Soli, Chor

ORCHESTRA

Piccolo, 2 Flutes, 2 Oboes,
2 Clarinets, 2 Bassoons, Contrabassoon;
4 Horns, 2 Trumpets, 3 Trombones;
Timpani, Percussion; Strings;
Soloists, Chorus

Aufführungsdauer / Duration: ca. 65 min.

Neben dieser Studienpartitur sind die Dirigierpartitur, das komplette Aufführungsmaterial, der Critical Commentary (BA 9009) und ein Klavierauszug (BA 9009a) erschienen.

In addition to the present Study Score the Full Score, the performance material, the Critical Commentary (BA 9009) and a Vocal Score (BA 9009a) are also published.

ISMN M-006-20432-8

INTRODUCTION

Beethoven's earliest significant ideas for a symphony in D minor date from 1812, when he was planning a set of three symphonies, including Nos. 7 and 8. Amongst the sketches for these are several ideas for a possible third work in the group. Three of these ideas are in D minor, although several other keys were considered at this stage. Towards the end of 1812, with his Eighth Symphony more or less completed, Beethoven seems to have abandoned the plan for another symphony, and ideas for new ones appeared very infrequently among his sketches during the next few years. Around the end of 1815 he jotted down a D minor theme that, with slight modifications, eventually appeared in the second movement of the Ninth Symphony; but there is no indication that it was intended for this purpose when it was first sketched.

Fresh impetus for a new symphony came in 1817, when the Philharmonic Society of London invited Beethoven to visit the city and bring two new symphonies with him. He seems to have responded by making a few sketches, in this and the following year, for the first movement of the Ninth Symphony, partly based on ideas jotted down previously; but he made little progress, and in the end he never made the planned visit to London. The sketches were then laid aside for several years while he concentrated on other projects, including sixteen sets of folksong variations (Opp. 105 and 107), the *Missa solemnis*, the Diabelli Variations and his last three piano sonatas (Opp. 109–111). While these works were in progress during 1819–21 he made very few sketches for the Ninth Symphony, but by summer 1822 his thoughts were beginning to turn to it again, and he wrote to the Philharmonic Society asking how much they would offer for a new symphony. Even before receiving a reply, he was making further sketches for the Ninth, as well as a few in E-flat major and C minor for a Tenth Symphony. On 10 November the Philharmonic Society resolved to offer him £50 for a new, unpublished symphony; and the following spring, once the Diabelli Variations were completed, he set to work in earnest on the Ninth.

By this stage Beethoven had decided to use passages from Schiller's 'Ode to Joy' for a grand, choral finale, and had even drafted its main theme. He had admired Schiller's poetry since his youth, and had contemplated setting the 'Ode to Joy' as early as 1793. He may even have done so a little later – there is a sketch from 1798 for one phrase, and Ferdinand Ries made a reference in 1803 to an apparently complete setting by Beethoven; but no such setting survives. In 1812 he considered incorporating individual lines from the poem into an overture (known as the 'Nameday' Overture), but this eventually appeared without any text. The idea of writing a symphony with choral finale first emerges in a sketch of 1818, but it was not until late 1822 that he decided on Schiller's text. From the fairly lengthy poem he selected the passages closest to his heart, such as 'Alle Menschen werden Brüder', which embodies his love for all humanity, and 'Über Sternen muß er wohnen', which reflects his deep devotion to an all-powerful and all-loving Deity who dwells beyond the created universe, and rearranged them in an order that best suited his purposes.

Beethoven's main work on the first two movements took place during May–July 1823, and he made good progress, despite a distressing eye infection which slowed him down considerably. The slow movement was evidently composed mainly during late summer, and the finale occupied him from then until about February 1824. The obvious next step was to organize a benefit concert, which could also include parts of his recently completed *Missa solemnis*; but Beethoven had lost faith in the Viennese public, where there was something of a craze for Rossini at the time, and considered having the premiere of the symphony in Berlin instead. However, he was won over by a petition presented by thirty of his admirers in Vienna, and plans were soon being made to hold the event there. There were many setbacks and disputes, concerning the venue, the performers, the prices, and the date, and there were difficulties with the censor over the proposed performance of music for the Mass in a theatre. The event was finally fixed for Friday 7 May, in the Kärntnerthor Theater, and the programme consisted of just three works, all by Beethoven: the Overture to *The Consecration of the House*; the Kyrie, Credo and Agnus Dei from the *Missa solemnis* (these movements had to be advertised as 'three grand hymns' to satisfy the censor); and the Ninth Symphony. Beethoven was by now too deaf to conduct, and so he merely set the speeds while the real conducting was entrusted to Michael Umlauf. The four soloists were Henriette Sontag (soprano), Caroline Unger (contralto), Anton Haitzinger (tenor) and Joseph Seipelt (bass). Although the enormous costs of mounting the concert prevented Beethoven from earning as much from it as he had expected, it was nevertheless a great success. There is a touching anecdote that at one point (probably after the second movement of the symphony), while the audience cheered wildly, Beethoven stood looking at the score with his back turned, too deaf to hear the applause, and had to be turned round by Unger to see it. The concert was repeated on 23 May with slight changes of programme, before a much smaller audience. The review in the *Allgemeine Musikalische Zeitung* reported that Beethoven's "inexhaustible genius had shown us a new world, revealing the magical secrets of a holy art that we had never before heard or imagined." (Nicholas Cook, *Beethoven Symphony No. 9* (1993), p. 23). The work was far less successful when tried out by the Philharmonic Society in London, however, and most of the members were completely bewildered by the finale. In fact it was not until the 1840s that the work gained widespread acceptance. Even today it remains a colossus among symphonies, with its great size and incredible inventiveness, complexity and power; yet these features are combined with a finale theme possessing such universal appeal that even the musically uninitiated can sense the joy it conveys.

Several innovations call for special comment, apart from the use of voices. The hushed, tremolando opening, with a single bare chord sustained for sixteen bars, already presages a work of vast dimensions, and the sound was widely imitated by Beethoven's successors. The use of B-flat for the second subject (I 80 and following) is noteworthy, for the key reappears in the slow movement and again in the finale (bar 331), providing long-distance tonal connections. The more remote key of B major similarly interrelates movements (I 108–15; III 91–8, notated as C-flat major; IV 836–42), each time appearing with a particularly gentle, ethereal sound. The start of the second movement (bars 1–8) is equally original. At first glance it seems to contain only one idea, but it actually contains two – a three-note motif and a sudden rest; and whereas the three-note motif becomes incorporated into the main theme (bar 9), to be extensively developed, the sudden rest is also treated motivically, being augmented (bars 7–8), tripled (bars 148–50, 156–8), and dramatically recapitulated as a closing device in the coda (bar 951). Beethoven has seemingly achieved the impossible, making something out of nothing. Another extraordinary idea is his grouping of bars into what might be called 'hyper-bars' of three units each, in the section marked 'Ritmo di tre battute' (bar 177). The third movement is remarkable for bringing together two seemingly unrelated themes (and the sketches confirm they had separate origins), in one of Beethoven's most profound and exquisite creations.

It is the finale, however, that takes pride of place, and although it might seem inconsistent with the rest of the work, Beethoven prepares for it very thoroughly. Its theme is foreshadowed in each of the first three movements (I 76–7, oboe and horn; II 416–8, oboe and clarinet; III 127–8, flute and oboe, marked *cantabile*), so that when the oboe first suggests the 'Freude' theme in the finale (IV 77–8) this instrument is actually quite familiar with it. To prepare for the choral music, Beethoven includes a lengthy instrumental introduction (bars 1–215), and he in turn prepares for these by including an introduction in each of the first three movements. And one final preparation for Schiller's Ode comes with the opening baritone solo (IV 216–36), using Beethoven's own words, 'O friends, not these tones!' The rest of the finale is essentially a set of free variations, somewhat modelled, as Beethoven himself said, on his own Choral Fantasia of 1808. The theme of a contrasting middle section ('Seid umschlungen', bar 595) is eventually combined with the 'Freude' theme in a magnificent double fugue (bar 654), and the unifying effect is completed by the reintroduction of the 'Turkish' instruments from the B-flat section for the closing passage (bars 851–end).

After finishing the Ninth Symphony, Beethoven made further sketches for the first movement of his Tenth, and by 1826 had a version of it worked out in his head. The sketches give a fairly clear indication of what he had in mind, and an 'artist's impression' of this movement has been made by the present writer from the sketches and other evidence. The sketches imply a much more intimate, personal work than the Ninth, and Beethoven probably intended a sharp contrast, like that between the Fifth and Sixth, or Seventh and Eighth. Thus even if Beethoven had completed his Tenth, it would surely not have overshadowed the all-embracing, cosmic grandeur of the Ninth, which forms a magnificent climax to his symphonic output.

Barry Cooper

PREFACE

Sources

A Autograph score, written in 1823–4 and mostly housed in the Staatsbibliothek zu Berlin – Preußischer Kulturbesitz (Musikabteilung), together with an autograph contrabassoon part; a few fragments, plus autograph trombone parts, are preserved in various other locations.

PX Nine manuscript string parts from the original material used at the first performance on 7 May 1824, housed in the Archiv der Gesellschaft der Musikfreunde, Vienna. All have a few corrections in Beethoven's hand.

B Copyist's score, with Beethoven's corrections, sent to London in December 1824 and housed in the British Library, London.

C Copyist's score used as engraver's copy (Stichvorlage) for **E**,**P**,**V** (see below), delivered to Schott on 16 January 1825 and housed in the archive of Schott Musik International, Mainz. This was the first score to be copied from **A**, and contains the bulk of Beethoven's revisions and corrections. Some pages were recopied, and are referred to as **C'**; these have very few corrections by Beethoven.

X Pages originally belonging to **C** which were superseded by **C'**. Most importantly, this includes twelve sheets which survive in the Staatsbibliothek zu Berlin – Preußischer Kulturbesitz; but much of **X** is lost.

CP Manuscript trombones and vocal parts, in the archive of Schott Musik International. These originally formed part of **PX**; the trombone parts contain corrections by Beethoven.

D Copyist's score, in the Stadtarchiv, Aachen; the volume containing the first three movements was corrected by Beethoven and sent to Aachen in March 1825.

DC Copyist's vocal score, in the Stadtarchiv, Aachen, corrected by Beethoven.

F Copyist's score, with Beethoven's corrections, in the Staatsbibliothek zu Berlin – Preußischer Kulturbesitz; presentation copy, with autograph dedication to King Friedrich Wilhelm III. It was delivered to the King in September 1826.

J Single autograph sheet, in the Staatsbibliothek zu Berlin – Preußischer Kulturbesitz, containing four new bars (I 255-8) missing in **A**.

K Autograph correction list, auctioned in London at Sotheby's in 1988 and now in private ownership.

L Revised version of **K**, in the hand of a copyist; housed in the Beethovenhaus, Bonn.

E,P,V First Edition of full score, parts and vocal score respectively, published by Schott in August 1826.

For a full account of these sources and their interrelationships, cf. Critical Commentary to BA 9009.

Specific editorial problems

Wherever possible, Beethoven's own notation, nomenclature, clefs, spelling of dynamic and tempo markings, and note-groupings have been retained. Many of these, therefore, will be found here for the first time since Beethoven's life-time; for instance, the inclusion (on which he was insistent, cf. Nottebohm, *Beethoveniana* (1872), pp.104–6) of the continuation marks = = = after every crescendo and diminuendo, which frequently serve the crucial purpose of distinguishing, for example, a *subito più f* from a *più f - - -*, which signifies a crescendo (e.g. I 527). Beethoven was equally punctilious about the retention of double stems (up and down) in his viola parts (the major surviving correction to his proof copy of the score of Symphony No.8, op.93 concerns this point), and this *divisi* notation, which Beethoven employed meticulously, has been strictly followed in our edition.

In some cases, where the effect is only a cosmetic one, Beethoven's notation has been modernized. His 𝄞𝄞 for horns and trumpets have been simplified to 𝄞; *Timpany* changed to *Timpani*; dynamic markings such as *for:*, *po:*, *ppmo:*, or *pianiss:*, especially *cres:*, and the rhythm 𝅗𝅥 𝅗𝅥 | . 𝅘𝅥 𝅗𝅥 , given their usual forms; and hairpins to the first note of a bar written

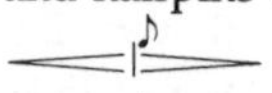

instead of Beethoven's frequent

. His nomenclature for horns varies from *primo, 2do, 3to e 4to* (as on the first page of **A**) to *2do corno* in III meaning 4.Cor, i.e. the second of the E♭ pair; but since this pairwise numbering is not used consistently, we adopt the usual modern convention. The clef of his bassoon parts is often capricious, depending on the exigencies of page-turns or deleted versions, and here we have preferred consistency. Soprano, alto and tenor parts are written in their eponymous clefs in the sources, and modernized here only in the interests of performance. Similarly, it was not Beethoven's practice to write double bars at key or tempo changes, but this modern convention has been allowed. Where the use of abbreviated forms such as 𝅗𝅥 is consistent, they have been retained; sometimes, to match adjacent bars or instruments, they have been changed to 𝅘𝅥𝅮𝅘𝅥𝅮𝅘𝅥𝅮𝅘𝅥𝅮. Finally, at I 301 Beethoven uses the (already in 1823 distinctly old-fashioned) notation / to signify *arpeggiando*; this again has been given its modern form.

Editorial insertions and emendations are distinguished by the use of either square brackets or (in the case of slurs, ties and hairpins) by broken type.

Slurs to and from grace notes

Beethoven never wrote slurs between grace notes and main notes, though they were invariably assumed in practice. We retain this convention, which is followed consistently in all the sources for op. 125, and applies identically to Nachschläge after trills. The figures in

IV 297–319 obey the same principle: though the Nachschläge are not written as grace notes, but as real ♬, this is still to be understood as trill notation, and thus played with slurs as a matter of course.

Woodwind slurs, etc. in shared staves

In the present score we have followed the usual modern convention: stems up and down necessitate a separate slur for each player, but where two notes share a single stem, one slur suffices for both players. Staccato is treated the same way, with one exception: where the two players are in unison (e.g. I 65 Cors), one stacc. has been held to suffice despite the two stems.

As one might expect, however, the early sources for op.125 are considerably more lax in their application of any such conventions, and the shared staves in **A** and **C** often cause ambiguity with regard to slurs for the 2nd players (e.g. IV 196 2.Fl).

Dynamics

It is of course well-known that a series of *f* markings in Beethoven represents repeated accentuation, and indeed it is virtually true to say that in such cases *f* is literally a shorthand for *sf*. In fact Beethoven never (in such a context) corrects a copyist's *f* to *sf*, or vice versa, so that the difference could indeed be held to be insignificant. Yet there is a psychological distinction between the two; and we have attempted to be as rigorous as possible in retaining this distinction. Nevertheless there are some passages (e.g. IV 463-70) where the original notation is so inconsistent between the two levels that a measure of logic has instead been sought, and only where *f* is locally consistent has it not been upgraded to the *sf* in other similar bars.

Beethoven occasionally uses a terminology that appears hardly to be documented in the literature of musical theory: *cresc .... il forte*, and (even more frequently) *il forte più forte*, sometimes written *il forte .... più forte ......* . We have placed our *f* to correspond with Beethoven's *il forte*, and this equivalence of nomenclature is confirmed in **B** at II 171, where Beethoven writes *f* in Vla, while Strings read *il for* in **A** and **C**.

A particular problem is presented by *pizzicato*. For some reason, such passages were held by Beethoven (and generally, indeed, other composers at this time, not excluding Berlioz) not to require any dynamic; in fact, the absence of a dynamic appears positively intentional, for there are many instances in Beethoven of *p* (in *arco*) being **altered** to *pizz.* Yet examples of *f pizzicato*, though rare in Beethoven, do exist, and gradations of dynamic in pizzicato are quite commonly found, cf. (in op.125) *cresc.* in II 322, IV 787, and *pizz. cres.* (Beethoven's handwriting in **C**) at I 266 Cb. At the same time one wonders what Beethoven's lower strings would have made of III 99, where after their *cresc.* the general (but for them, unmarked) *sub. p* is hardly expected. IV 238/40 originally read *f* in **A**, altered to *pizz.* (cf. Critical Commentary to BA 9009), but the marking *pizz. p* was allowed to remain in 241, implying that 238/40 were indeed possibly intended to be played a little louder. The most problematic places in Beethoven are those where the prevailing dynamic appears to be *f*, yet the pizzicato entries obstinately refuse to indicate anything (e.g. Symphony No.5 II 7; Piano Concerto No.4 III 61). Clearly such extreme ambiguity cannot be acceptable in a modern performing edition – for some decades, indeed, there was even a controversy as to whether Beethoven might have intended the *pizz.* in III 157 to be played *f* – and we have supplied such dynamics as are necessary, clearly notated as editorial additions.

Beethoven's diminuendo hairpins, though less frequent than Schubert's, are no less problematic. Like Schubert's, they are written long, and often signify something closer to an accent; unlike Schubert's (which are generally placed centrally above or below the note) they tend to start under the note, thus looking especially like diminuendos. There is nowadays no adequate way to notate unambiguously such a sign which is, by its very nature, ambiguous. Depending on context, it will signify differing degrees of both accent and diminuendo together. We have rendered these as accents, but it must be emphasized that very often (e.g. especially IV 254, 753, 810–1, 833–4) these accents are to be understood as containing a substantial element of diminuendo. (Cf. particularly note on II 198–208 in the Critical Commentary to BA 9009.)

Punkte and Striche

Beethoven was said (cf. Nottebohm, op. cit., pp.107–25) to be punctilious about the difference between Punkte and Striche (dots and dashes), and a letter of August 1825 to Karl Holz (Emily Anderson, *The Letters of Beethoven* (1961), No.1421), in which Beethoven gives the firm instruction that " and  are not identical", is cited as evidence of this. Yet it is nowadays generally agreed that any distinction in Beethoven sources between the two is only identifiable so sporadically as to be impossible to reflect in a new edition with any degree of logic or consistency. To this there is one exception: the portato, which of course must always be accompanied by Punkte. Apart from portato, then, we show Beethoven's staccato signs always as Striche, and this is precisely corroborated by his copious corrections (also quoted by Nottebohm, op. cit. pp.107–9) to the first performance parts of the Allegretto of the Symphony No.7 (op.92), viz:

 (etc.).

Specific problems of the Finale: orthography and punctuation of Schiller's text

Beethoven was extremely hasty, and consequently careless, where punctuation is concerned. For the present edition, four early printings of Schiller's 'An die Freude' were examined, as follows:

SA First edition of 'An die Freude', published in *Thalia*, a periodical edited by Schiller, Leipzig, 1786.

SB *Gedichte von Friederich Schiller*, Leipzig, 1803.

SC *Gedichte von Friedrich Schiller*, Kreuznach, 1804.

SD *Friedrich von Schillers sämmtliche Werke*, Stuttgart & Tübingen, 1812. (First Complete Edition.)
as well as an identical reprint of **SD** ('Zweite unveränderte Auflage') of 1818.

The main differences between the four texts are as follows:

1) An earlier version of lines 6–7 is found only in **SA**, viz:
was der Mode Schwerd getheilt;
Bettler werden Fürstenbrüder,
whereas **SB**, **SC** and **SD** give the revised version:
was die Mode streng getheilt;
Alle Menschen werden Brüder,
2) **SA** and **SB** give *siegen*; **SC** and **SD** have *Siegen*.
3) **SA**, **SB** and **SC** give the obsolete *Ahndest*; **SD** has *Ahnest*.

Comparison with the sources for op.125 show that the text Beethoven used was probably **SD** or a reprint of it; and this text therefore forms our starting-point. We have, however, preferred two details in which Beethoven's text was both in itself consistent, and in agreement with **SA**: *eine Seele* (**SB**, **SC**, **SD** *Eine Seele*), and the absence of a comma after *umschlungen* (only **SD** has this comma).

All the available versions of Schiller agree that there are dashes after *Ja* and *Brüder*, but this punctuation could risk confusion in a musical score where the dash has another significance entirely, and we have accepted comma and exclamation marks respectively from **E**. We have also followed **E**'s punctuation in isolated outbursts of *Freude!* (bars 238/40, 664, etc.), and portions of sentence such as bars 767–81. However, Beethoven furnished his introductory recitative with no fewer than four exclamation marks in **A** (in bars 219/21/9/36); we have restored this in 236 (since punctuation was omitted entirely in **X**), but followed **C** and later sources in 219/29.

Obsolete forms such as *seyd*, *neñt* and *getheilt* have been modernized without comment.

Vocal slurs

Beethoven's vocal slurs by no means always coincide with changes of syllable, but are often shorter; they have real significance with regard to phrasing, and consequently have (contrary to normal conventions) to be granted their independence from the underlay. A typical example of this is bars 895–8. However, there are so few examples where his slurs are longer than the syllables that these can virtually all be dismissed as errors. These usually occur where the words appear to have been entered subsequently; indeed, most are present only in **A**, and were probably deleted in **X**. However, just one appears to have real purpose and has been retained; this is bar 840 (Soprano).

Vocal dynamics

In **A**, Beethoven often writes dynamics only in the Soprano line. It is patently clear from the contexts that a general dynamic for all voices is intended; and he almost always remembers to repair the omissions in **C** (e.g. bar 282). Though he occasionally forgets (e.g. 280), we have allowed the principle to operate without comment in these most obvious cases. However, this clearly does not apply in 798–800 (Solo Soprano); and in cases of doubt (such as, therefore, 797, or 742) we have adhered strictly to the text in the sources.

Rehearsal letters

In order to render our Edition as convenient and practical as possible, we have retained the traditional rehearsal letters, as universally adopted in performing editions of the Beethoven Symphonies. It should be emphasized, however, that these are in no sense authentic, originating only some decades after Beethoven's death. They are therefore presented as an adjunct to, rather than as an integral part of, this Urtext Edition.

Acknowledgements

I record here with pleasure all those to whom grateful thanks are due: first and foremost, to Caroline Brown and Stephen Neiman of The Hanover Band, who provided the initial impulse and many years' funding for my Beethoven researches.

The staff of the Westminster Music Library, London and David Royal of the London Borough of Lambeth Library Service have been untiringly helpful in their searches for many articles from myriad journals, and I thank them for their patience and persistence. Thanks, too, to the staffs of the many libraries in which I conducted my research: both houses of the Staatsbibliothek zu Berlin – Preußischer Kulturbesitz; the Archiv der Gesellschaft der Musikfreunde, Vienna; the British Library, London; the Library of the Royal College of Music, London; the Stadtarchiv, Aachen; and Schott Musik International, Mainz, to whom I owe a very special debt of gratitude. In addition, I am beholden to several individuals for help of one kind or another in the course of my research: Otto Biba, Sieghard Brandenburg, Nicholas Cook, Barry Cooper, William Drabkin, John Eliot Gardiner, Roy Goodman, Stephen Johnson, H.C. Robbins Landon, Sir Charles Mackerras, Graham Nattrass, Sir Simon Rattle, Nigel Simeone, Peter Stadlen and John Warrack.

Particular thanks must also go to The British Academy, whose funding of the final stages of my research enabled the work to be completed.

Finally, I am especially grateful both to my mother, Pauline Del Mar, and to my wife, Annabel Teh Gallop, for endless help and patience in the preparation of the typescript of the Critical Commentary.

Jonathan Del Mar

EINLEITUNG

Beethovens früheste ernstzunehmende Ideen für eine Symphonie in d-moll stammen aus dem Jahr 1812. Damals plante er eine Gruppe von drei Symphonien, zu der die Siebte und die Achte gehören sollten. In deren Skizzen finden sich mehrere Ideen, die vielleicht für das dritte Werk der Gruppe vorgesehen waren. Drei dieser Gedanken stehen in d-moll; allerdings wurden in diesem Stadium auch mehrere andere Tonarten erwogen. Gegen Ende des Jahres 1812, als die Achte Symphonie im wesentlichen fertig war, scheint Beethoven den Plan zu einer weiteren Symphonie aufgegeben zu haben. In den darauf folgenden Jahren tauchen in seinen Skizzen nur sehr selten Ideen für neue Symphonien auf. Ungefähr Ende 1815 notierte er ein d-moll-Thema, das mit leichten Veränderungen schließlich in den zweiten Satz der Neunten Symphonie Eingang fand. Es deutet jedoch nichts darauf hin, daß es bei seiner ersten schriftlichen Fixierung bereits für diesen Zweck bestimmt war.

Frische Impulse für eine neue Symphonie kamen 1817, als die Londoner Philharmonische Gesellschaft Beethoven einlud, die Stadt zu besuchen und zwei neue Symphonien mitzubringen. Wohl daraufhin hat Beethoven in diesem und dem folgenden Jahr ein paar Skizzen für den ersten Satz der Neunten Symphonie notiert, die sich zum Teil an früheren Ideen orientieren. Doch er kam nicht recht voran, und letztlich ist aus dem geplanten London-Besuch nichts geworden. Beethoven ließ die Skizzen mehrere Jahre liegen und widmete sich in der Zeit hauptsächlich anderen Projekten, so den *6 variierten Themen* op. 105 und den *10 variierten Themen* op. 107, der *Missa solemnis*, den *Diabelli-Variationen* und den letzten drei Klaviersonaten (op. 109, 110 und 111). Während er 1819–1821 an diesen Werken arbeitete, notierte er nur sehr wenig Material für die Neunte Symphonie, aber im Sommer 1822 befaßte er sich erneut mit ihr und fragte die Philharmonische Gesellschaft in London, wieviel sie für eine neue Symphonie zu zahlen bereit sei. Noch ehe die Antwort eintraf, brachte er weitere Skizzen zur Neunten zu Papier sowie einige weitere in Es-dur und c-moll für eine Zehnte Symphonie. Am 10. November entschloß sich die Philharmonische Gesellschaft, Beethoven für eine neue, unveröffentlichte Symphonie 50 Pfund anzubieten. Im folgenden Frühjahr, als die *Diabelli-Variationen* beendet waren, begann er ernsthaft mit der Arbeit an der Neunten.

In diesem Stadium hatte sich Beethoven entschlossen, Verse aus Schillers Ode *An die Freude* als Text für ein großes Chorfinale zu benutzen. Das Hauptthema war sogar schon entworfen. Seit seiner Jugend ein Bewunderer von Schillers Dichtung, hatte Beethoven bereits 1793 an eine Vertonung der Ode *An die Freude* gedacht. Vielleicht ist daraus wenig später tatsächlich etwas geworden – es gibt nämlich aus dem Jahre 1798 die Skizze zu einem entsprechenden Satz, und Ferdinand Ries erwähnte 1803 eine anscheinend vollständige Vertonung des Textes von Beethoven, die allerdings nicht überliefert ist. 1812 erwog Beethoven, einzelne Verse aus dem Schillerschen Gedicht in eine Ouvertüre zu integrieren (es handelte sich um die später *Zur Namensfeier* betitelte Ouvertüre), aber das Werk erschien dann doch ohne Text. Die Idee zu einer Symphonie mit Chorfinale taucht zum ersten Mal in einer Skizze aus dem Jahre 1818 auf, indes entschied sich Beethoven erst Ende 1822 für Schillers Text. Aus dem recht langen Gedicht wählte er solche Stellen aus, die seinen Gefühlen entsprachen, z. B. „Alle Menschen werden Brüder", Ausdruck seiner Liebe zur ganzen Menschheit, und „Über Sternen muß er wohnen", Verkörperung seiner tiefen Ehrfurcht vor einer allmächtigen, alliebenden Gottheit jenseits des erschaffenen Alls, und er ordnete sie so an, wie es seinen Vorstellungen entsprach.

Die Hauptarbeit an den ersten beiden Sätzen ging von Mai bis Juli 1823. Trotz einer quälenden Augeninfektion, die sein Schaffenstempo beträchtlich drosselte, kam Beethoven gut voran. Der langsame Satz wurde offensichtlich zum größten Teil im Spätsommer komponiert, und das Finale beschäftigte Beethoven anschließend bis etwa Februar 1824. Der nächste Schritt wäre nun die Vorbereitung eines Benefizkonzerts gewesen, bei dem auch Teile der unlängst vollendeten *Missa solemnis* hätten erklingen können. Aber Beethoven besaß kein Vertrauen mehr in das Wiener Publikum, das sich damals dem Rossini-Taumel hingab, und so dachte er daran, die Premiere der Symphonie nach Berlin zu vergeben. Dann aber stimmten ihn dreißig seiner Bewunderer in Wien mit einer Bittschrift um, und bald begann man mit der Organisation der Uraufführung.

Es gab viele Rückschläge und Kontroversen hinsichtlich des Veranstaltungsorts, der Mitwirkenden, der Eintrittspreise, des Datums, und es gab Schwierigkeiten mit dem Zensor, weil Musik für die Messe in einem Theater gegeben werden sollte. Schließlich wurde die Aufführung für Freitag, den 7. Mai, im Kärntnertor-Theater angesetzt. Auf dem Programm standen nur drei Werke, alle von Beethoven: die Ouvertüre *Die Weihe des Hauses*, Kyrie, Credo und Agnus Dei aus der *Missa solemnis* (diese Sätze mußten als „drei große Hymnen" deklariert werden, um den Zensor zufriedenzustellen), und die Neunte Symphonie. Beethoven konnte wegen seiner fortgeschrittenen Taubheit nicht selbst dirigieren, sondern gab nur immer zu Beginn das Tempo an, und Kapellmeister Michael Umlauf oblag die eigentliche Leitung. Die vier Solisten waren Henriette Sontag (Sopran), Caroline Unger (Alt), Anton Haitzinger (Tenor) und Joseph Seipelt (Baß). Auch wenn Beethoven der hohen Veranstaltungskosten wegen an dem Konzert nicht soviel verdiente, wie er gehofft hatte, war es doch ein großer Erfolg. Eine bewegende Anekdote hält folgende Szene fest: An einer Stelle (wahrscheinlich nach dem zweiten Satz der Symphonie) brach das Publikum in Jubel aus. Beethoven wandte ihm den Rücken zu, blickte auf die Partitur und hörte den Applaus nicht. Sanft wendete Caroline Unger ihn dem Publikum zu, und nun sah er den Beifall. Am 23. Mai wurde das Konzert mit geringen Programmänderungen vor einer viel kleineren Zuhörerschaft wiederholt. In der Besprechung der *Allgemeinen Musikalischen Zeitung* heißt es, daß Beethovens „unerschöpfliches Genie uns eine neue Welt erschloss, nie gehörte, nie geahndete Wunder-Geheimnisse der heiligen Kunst entschleyerte!" (*AMZ* XXVI Nr. 24, Sp. 438)

Längst nicht so gut kam das Werk bei einer Aufführung der Londoner Philharmonischen Gesellschaft an; namentlich das Finale verwirrte die meisten ihrer Mitglieder völlig. Tatsächlich fand das Werk erst nach 1840 weite Verbreitung. Bis heute ist die Neunte mit ihren Ausmaßen, ihrer unglaublichen Einfallsfülle, Vielschichtigkeit und Kraft ein Koloß unter den Symphonien geblieben. Andererseits aber verbinden sich diese Züge mit einem Finalthema von so umfassender Wirkung, daß sogar der musikalische Laie fühlen kann, welche Freude es ausstrahlt.

Abgesehen vom Hinzutreten von Soli und Chor bringt die Symphonie einige Neuerungen, zu denen noch einige Erläuterungen gegeben werden sollen. In der gedämpften Tremolando-Einleitung mit der sechzehn Takte lang ertönenden leeren Quinte kündigt sich bereits ein Werk von riesigen Dimensionen an, und der Klang ist in der Nachfolge Beethovens viel imitiert worden. Die Verwendung der Tonart B-dur für das zweite Thema (I 80ff.) verdient Beachtung, weil die Tonart im langsamen Satz sowie im Finale (Takt 331) wiederkehrt, womit über lange Strecken hinweg Tonartbeziehungen hergestellt werden. Auch das entferntere H-dur schafft Beziehungen zwischen einzelnen Sätzen (I 108–115; III 91–98, als Ces-dur notiert; IV 836–842) und verbindet sich dabei jedesmal mit einem besonders weichen, ätherischen Klang. Auch der Beginn des zweiten Satzes (Takt 1–8) ist in vergleichbarer Weise originell. Auf den ersten Blick scheint er nur einen einzigen Gedanken zu enthalten. In Wirklichkeit sind es aber zwei: ein Dreiton-Motiv und eine plötzliche Pause. Während das Dreiton-Motiv in das Hauptthema eingebaut wird (Takt 9) und dann umfassende Verarbeitung erfährt, gewinnt auch die jähe Pause motivische Bedeutung: Sie wird verdoppelt (Takte 7–8), verdreifacht (Takt 148–150, 156–158) und in der

Coda dramatisch als Schlußgeste wieder aufgenommen (Takt 951). Wie es scheint, ist Beethoven das Unmögliche gelungen – er hat aus nichts etwas gemacht. Ein anderer, außergewöhnlicher Einfall ist die Zusammenfassung von Takten zu Dreiergruppen – man könnte diese als „Über-Takte" bezeichnen – in dem Abschnitt mit der Anweisung „Ritmo di tre battute" (Takt 177). Das Außerordentliche des dritten Satzes besteht darin, daß Beethoven hier zwei Themen, die anscheinend nicht verwandt sind (und die Skizzen bestätigen ihre unterschiedlichen Wurzeln), zu einer seiner tiefsten und erlesensten Schöpfungen zusammenführt.

Den Ehrenplatz nimmt allerdings das Finale ein. Auch wenn dieser Satz nicht recht zum übrigen Werk zu passen scheint, so bereitet Beethoven ihn doch sehr gründlich vor: Das Thema des Finales klingt in jedem der ersten drei Sätze an (I 76–77, Oboe und Horn; II 416–418, Oboe und Klarinette; III 127–128, Flöte und Oboe, mit der Vortragsbezeichnung *cantabile*), so daß die Oboe, wenn sie im Schlußsatz zum ersten Mal das „Freude"-Thema andeutet (IV 77–78), mit ihm bereits gut vertraut ist. Als Vorbereitung für den Choreinsatz benutzt Beethoven eine lange Instrumentaleinleitung (Takt 1 bis 215), und dies wiederum ist dadurch vorbereitet, daß jeder der ersten drei Sätze mit einer Einleitung beginnt. Eine letzte Einstimmung auf Schillers Ode bewirkt das eröffnende Bariton-Solo (IV 216–236) „O Freunde, nicht diese Töne!" (auf Worte Beethovens). Das eigentliche Finale ist im wesentlichen eine Reihe von freien Variationen, denen teilweise, wie Beethoven selber sagte, seine Chorfantasie von 1808 als Modell gedient hat. Das Thema des kontrastierenden Mittelteils („Seid umschlungen", Takt 595) wird schließlich in einer großartigen Doppelfuge (Takt 654) mit dem „Freude"-Thema verknüpft, und das Wiederauftreten der „türkischen" Instrumente aus dem B-dur-Abschnitt im Schlußteil (Takte 851 bis Ende) rundet die vereinheitlichende Wirkung ab.

Nach Vollendung der Neunten machte Beethoven weitere Skizzen zum ersten Satz seiner Zehnten Symphonie, und 1826 hatte er eine ausgearbeitete Fassung im Kopf. Aus den Skizzen ergibt sich ziemlich klar, was er sich vorstellte, und der Verfasser hat nach den Skizzen und anderem Material eine „Umrißzeichnung" dieses Satzes angefertigt. In den Skizzen deutet sich ein viel intimeres, persönlicheres Werk an, als es in der Neunten vorliegt. Wahrscheinlich beabsichtigte Beethoven einen scharfen Kontrast, wie er zwischen der Fünften und Sechsten oder der Siebten und Achten Symphonie besteht. Hätte er seine Zehnte geschrieben, hätte er damit sicherlich nicht die allumfassende, kosmische Größe der Neunten übertroffen, dieses herrliche Gipfelwerk seines symphonischen Schaffens.

Barry Cooper
(Übersetzung: Thomas M. Höpfner)

VORWORT

Quellen

A Autographe Partitur, geschrieben zwischen 1823 und 1824, zum größten Teil, zusammen mit der autographen Kontrafagottstimme im Besitz der Staatsbibliothek zu Berlin – Preußischer Kulturbesitz (Musikabteilung). Weitere Teile des Autographs, einschließlich autographer Posaunenstimmen, werden an verschiedenen anderen Orten aufbewahrt.

PX Neun handschriftliche Streicherstimmen aus dem Material der Erstaufführung vom 7. Mai 1824, im Besitz des Archivs der Gesellschaft der Musikfreunde in Wien. Alle Stimmen enthalten in geringer Zahl Korrekturen von Beethovens Hand.

B Partiturkopie mit Korrekturen Beethovens. Die Kopie wurde im Dezember 1824 nach London gesandt und befindet sich heute in der British Library, London.

C Stichvorlage für **E**, **P**, **V** (s.u.), eine Partiturkopie, die am 16. Januar 1825 an den Verlag Schott in Mainz geschickt wurde, heute im Besitz des Archivs von Schott Musik International. **C**, die erste Partiturkopie, die unmittelbar auf **A** zurückgeht, enthält die Hauptmenge von Beethovens Korrekturen und Revisionen. Einige Seiten wurden nochmals geschrieben (Quelle **C′**); sie enthalten nur wenige Korrekturen Beethovens.

X Zwölf Einzelblätter aus **C**, die durch **C′** ersetzt wurden, im Besitz der Staatsbibliothek zu Berlin – Preußischer Kulturbesitz. Ein Großteil weiterer zu **X** gehörender Blätter ist verschollen.

CP Handschriftliche Posaunen- und Vokalstimmen, im Besitz des Archivs von Schott Musik International, Mainz. Sie gehörten ursprünglich zu **PX**; die Posaunenstimmen enthalten Korrekturen Beethovens.

D Partiturkopie im Besitz des Stadtarchivs Aachen; der Band mit den ersten drei Sätzen des Werkes enthält Korrekturen Beethovens. Er wurde im März 1825 nach Aachen geschickt.

DC Handschriftlicher, von Beethoven korrigierter Klavierauszug, im Besitz des Stadtarchivs Aachen.

F Widmungskopie mit autographer Widmung an König Friedrich Wilhelm III. von Preußen und Korrekturen Beethovens, im Besitz der Staatsbibliothek zu Berlin – Preußischer Kulturbesitz. Sie wurde im September 1826 an den König übersandt.

J Autographes Einzelblatt, das vier neue Takte des ersten Satzes (I 255–258) enthält, die in **A** fehlen, im Besitz der Staatsbibliothek zu Berlin – Preußischer Kulturbesitz.

K Autographe Korrekturliste, versteigert 1988 bei Sotheby's in London, heute in Privatbesitz.

L Kopistenabschrift von **K** in revidierter Fassung, im Besitz des Beethoven-Hauses Bonn.

E,P,V Erstausgabe von Partitur, Stimmen und Klavierauszug, erschienen im August 1826 bei Schott in Mainz.

Einen ausführlichen Bericht über die Quellen und deren Abhängigkeiten vermittelt der Critical Commentary zu BA 9009.

Spezielle Editionsprobleme

Wo immer möglich, wurden Eigenheiten von Beethovens Notation, seine Nomenklatur, Schlüssel, die Schreibweise von Dynamik und Tempobezeichnungen sowie die Notierung von Notengruppierungen beibehalten. Vieles davon erscheint in der vorliegenden Edition erstmals seit Beethovens Lebenszeit. Dies gilt beispielsweise für die Verlängerungszeichen = = = nach jedem crescendo und diminuendo (auf die Beethoven nach Nottebohm, *Beethoveniana*, 1872, S. 104–106, hartnäckig bestanden hat). Sie bilden oftmals wesentliche Unterscheidungskriterien, z.B. zwischen einem *subito più f* und einem *più f* - - - in der Bedeutung eines crescendo (z.B. in I 527). Von ähnlich peinlicher Genauigkeit war Beethoven bei der Setzung von doppelter Behalsung (auf- und abwärts) im Viola-Part (der Großteil der überlieferten Korrekturen im Korrekturabzug der Partitur von Symphonie Nr. 8 op. 93 betrifft diesen Punkt); diese *divisi*-Notation, die Beethoven mit peinlicher Genauigkeit anwendet, wird in der vorliegenden Edition strikt beibehalten.

In einigen Fällen, in denen Beethovens Notation lediglich kosmetische Abweichungen betrifft, wurde modernisiert. Statt der 𝄞𝄞 bei Hörnern und Trompeten wurde 𝄞 gesetzt; die Bezeichnung *Timpany* wurde geändert in *Timpani*; dynamische Bezeichnungen wie *for:*, *po:*, *ppmo:*, oder *pianiss:*, insbesondere *cres:*, sowie die altertümliche Notation von Augmentationspunkten 𝅗𝅥 𝅗𝅥 |. ♩ 𝅗𝅥 erscheinen in der heute gebräuchlichen Form. Crescendo-Decrescendo-Gabeln zur ersten Note eines Taktes erscheinen in der Form  statt der bei Beethoven häufigen Schreibung . Beethovens Zählung der Hörner variiert von *primo, 2do, 3to e 4to* (auf der ersten Notenseite von **A**) zu *2do corno* in III in der Bedeutung von Horn IV, zu verstehen als zweites Horn des Es-Hörner-Paares. Aber da diese paarweise Zählung der Hörner nicht konsequent durchgeführt ist, verwenden wir die moderne Bezeichnung. Die Schlüsselung der Fagotte ist in den Quellen oftmals kapriziös und hängt von der Einrichtung von Seitenwendern ab oder geht auf verworfene Fassungen zurück; in der vorliegenden Edition wurde die Schlüsselung vereinheitlicht. Sopran, Alt und Tenor sind in den Quellen in den den Stimmlagen entsprechenden C-Schlüsseln notiert; im Hinblick auf die musikalische Praxis verwendet die vorliegende Edition moderne Schlüssel. Beethoven setzt prinzipiell keine Doppel-Taktstriche vor Schlüssel- oder Tempowechsel; sie entsprechen aber moderner Notation und wurden in der vorliegenden Edition eingeführt. Abbreviaturen wie 𝅗𝅥 wurden immer dann übernommen, wenn sie in den Quellen durchgehend konsequent vorkommen; gelegentlich wurden sie jedoch zur Angleichung an andere Instrumente oder unmittelbar benachbarter Takte aufgelöst (♫♫). Schließlich (I 301) verwendet Beethoven die (bereits 1823 eindeutig antiquierte) Notation / zur Bezeichnung eines *arpeggiando*; die vorliegende Edition verwendet hierfür die moderne Notationsform. Herausgeberzutaten und Emendationen werden gekennzeichnet, und zwar durch eckige Klammern oder (im Falle von Artikulations- und Haltebögen sowie Gabeln) durch Strichelung.

Bögen bei Ziernoten

Beethoven schrieb niemals Bögen zwischen Ziernoten und Hauptnoten, obwohl sie in der Praxis durchgehend vorausgesetzt werden müssen. Die vorliegende Edition folgt Beethovens Notation, die im übrigen in sämtlichen Quellen von op. 125 durchgehend anzutreffen ist; sie gilt in gleicher Weise für Nachschlagsnoten nach Trillern. Die Figuren in IV 297–319 gehorchen demselben Prinzip: wenngleich die Nachschläge nicht als Ziernoten sondern als normale ♬ notiert sind, so sind die Stellen doch als Triller-Notation zu verstehen und selbstverständlich gebunden zu spielen.

Bögen bei Holzbläsern etc. in geteilten Systemen

Die vorliegende Edition folgt der gebräuchlichen modernen Notation: getrennte Halsung (auf- und abwärts) verlangt eigene Bögen für jedes Instrument, doch wenn zwei Noten zusammengehalst sind, steht für beide Instrumente nur ein Bogen. Staccato-Bezeichnungen werden genauso behandelt, mit einer Ausnahme: bei unisono beider Instrumente und doppelter Behalsung (z.B. Hörner in I 65) steht nur ein Staccato-Zeichen. Wie zu erwarten, sind jedoch die frühen Quellen von op. 125 in der strikten Anwendung dieser Notation eher nachlässig, und die Notation geteilter Systeme in **A** und **C** führt bei der Bogensetzung im zweiten (unteren) Instrument oftmals zu Mehrdeutigkeiten (z.B. Flöten in IV 196).

Dynamik

Es ist bekannt, daß eine Folge von *f*-Zeichen bei Beethoven wiederholte Akzentuierung meint, und es entspricht durchaus den Tatsachen, daß in solchen Fällen das *f* nichts anderes als eine abgekürzte Schreibweise für *sf* darstellt. Beethoven hat in solchen Fällen niemals ein vom Kopisten notiertes *f* in ein *sf* korrigiert oder umgekehrt, so daß der Unterschied in der Tat als unerheblich anzusehen ist. Es gibt allerdings einen psychologischen Unterschied zwischen beiden Zeichen, und deshalb wurde in der vorliegenden Edition versucht, diese Unterscheidung so rigoros wie nur eben möglich durchzuführen. Nichtsdestoweniger gibt es einige Passagen (z.B. in IV 463–470), in denen die Originalnotation derartig zwischen beiden Bezeichnungen schwankt, daß ein gewisses Maß an Logik in der Zeichensetzung gefunden werden mußte. Nur wo das *f* innerhalb eines bestimmten Bereichs konsequent gesetzt ist, wurde es nicht in ein *sf* analog anderer ähnlicher Takte korrigiert.

Beethoven verwendet gelegentlich eine Terminologie, die man in der musiktheoretischen Literatur vergeblich suchen dürfte: *cresc ... il forte,* und (noch häufiger) *il forte più forte,* manchmal geschrieben *il forte ...più forte ...* . In der vorliegenden Edition entspricht ein *f* dem Beethovenschen *il forte* , eine Entsprechung der Bezeichnungen, die in Quelle **B**, II 171, belegt ist: Beethoven schreibt dort ein *f* in der Vla, während die Streicher in **A** und **C** die Bezeichnung *il for* tragen.

Ein besonderes Problem bildet das *pizzicato.* Aus gewissen Gründen kann angenommen werden, daß Beethoven (und generell andere zeitgenössische Komponisten, Berlioz nicht ausgenommen) in solchen Passagen keinerlei Dynamik vorsieht, eine Einschätzung, die dadurch positiv bestätigt wird, daß es bei Beethoven viele Fälle gibt, in denen ein ursprüngliches *p* in einer arco-Passage zu einem *pizz.* **umgeschrieben** wurde. Dennoch gibt es bei Beethoven Beispiele für *f pizzicato,* wenn auch selten, während dynamische Abstufungen recht häufig anzutreffen sind, z.B. (in op. 125) ein *cresc.* in II 322, IV 787, und ein *pizz. cresc.* (von Beethovens Hand in **C**) in I 266, Cb. In diesem Zusammenhang fragt man sich, wie sich Beethovens tiefe Streicher bei III 99 verhalten haben mögen, wo auf deren *cresc.* ein generelles (in ihren Stimmen aber nicht eigens bezeichnetes) *sub. p* ziemlich unerwartet folgt. IV 238 und 240 waren in **A** ursprünglich mit *f* bezeichnet, was später zu *pizz.* wurde (vgl. Critical Commentary zu BA 9009), aber die Bezeichnung *pizz. p* für 241 ist unverändert geblieben, was wohl nur bedeuten kann, daß 238 und 240 in der Tat ein wenig lauter gespielt werden sollen als 241 ff. Die problematischsten Stellen sind bei Beethoven solche, in denen *f* als Grunddynamik vorzuherrschen scheint, die pizzicato-Angaben jedoch alle Bezeichnungen beharrlich außer Kraft setzen (z.B. 5. Symphonie II 7, 4. Klavierkonzert III 61). Natürlich sind solche Mehrdeutigkeiten in einer modernen praktischen Urtext-Ausgabe gänzlich unakzeptabel – in der Tat gab es vor einigen Jahrzehnten sogar eine Kontroverse über die Frage, ob Beethoven das *pizz.* in III 157 *f* ausgeführt wissen will –, und darum wurden solche dynamischen Bezeichnungen wo notwendig ergänzt, jedoch als editorische Zusätze kenntlich gemacht.

Beethovens Diminuendo-Gabeln sind, wenn sie auch etwas seltener vorkommen als bei Schubert, nicht weniger problematisch. Wie bei Schubert sind sie lang geschrieben und nähern sich oftmals dem Akzentzeichen. Aber anders als bei Schubert (wo sie generell in der Mitte ober- oder unterhalb der Note plaziert sind), neigen sie bei Beethoven dazu, unter der Note zu beginnen und gewinnen so ganz besonders das Aussehen eines Diminuendo. Es gibt heute keine Möglichkeit, solche Zeichen so mehrdeutig in moderne Notation umzusetzen, wie sie ihrer Natur nach gemeint sind. Je nach dem musikalischen Zusammenhang bezeichnet es verschiedene Abstufungen zwischen Akzent und Diminuendo und umgekehrt. Wir geben sie als Akzente wieder, doch sei mit Nachdruck darauf hingewiesen, daß diese Akzente sehr oft (z.B. ganz besonders in IV 254, 753, 810–811, 833–834) so zu interpretieren sind, daß sie substantiell auch Elemente eines Diminuendo in sich tragen (vgl. insbesondere die Bemerkung zu II 198–208 im Critical Commentary zu BA 9009.)

Punkte und Striche

Von Beethoven wurde behauptet (vgl. Nottebohm, a.a.O., S. 107–125), er sei peinlich genau hinsichtlich der Unterscheidung von Staccato-Punkten und -Strichen gewesen. Als Beweis dafür wird ein Brief Beethovens an Karl Holz vom August 1825 angeführt (Sieghard Brandenburg, *Ludwig van Beethoven: Briefwechsel. Gesamtausgabe*, 1996, Nr. 2032), in dem Beethoven die klare Auskunft erteilt, daß 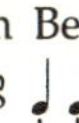 und  nicht dasselbe seien. Es besteht jedoch heute allgemeine Übereinkunft darin, daß aus Beethovens Quellen eine definitive Unterscheidung zwischen beiden Zeichen nur sehr sporadisch abgeleitet werden kann, so daß für eine moderne Neuausgabe in dieser Hinsicht keinerlei Basis für eine systematische Anwendung beider Zeichen gegeben ist, die auch nur in etwa einen Anspruch auf Logik oder Konsequenz erheben könnte. Abgesehen vom Portato, das immer mit Punkten wiedergegeben wird, erscheinen in der vorliegenden Edition Beethovens Staccato-Angaben grundsätzlich als Striche. Diese Praxis erfährt übrigens durch Beethovens eigene reichhaltige Korrekturen im Erstaufführungsmaterial der 7. Sinfonie op. 92 eine deutliche Bestätigung:  (etc.) (vgl. auch Nottebohm, a.a.O., S. 107–109).

Spezielle Probleme im Finale: Orthographie und Interpunktion in Schillers Text

Beethovens Schreibung von Interpunktion macht einen hastigen und in Folge davon sorglosen Eindruck. Für die vorliegende Edition wurden vier Frühdrucke von Schillers Ode *An die Freude* herangezogen:

SA Erstdruck von *An die Freude*, erschienen in der *Thalia*, einem Jahrbuch, das von Schiller 1786 in Leipzig herausgegeben wurde

SB *Gedichte von Friederich Schiller*, Leipzig 1803

SC *Gedichte von Friedrich Schiller*, Kreuznach 1804

SD *Friedrich von Schillers sämmtliche Werke*, Stuttgart & Tübingen 1812 (erste Gesamtausgabe)
Ebenfalls eingesehen wurde die „Zweite unveränderte Auflage" 1818 von **SD**.

Die wesentlichen Abweichungen zwischen den vier Texten sind die folgenden:

1) Eine frühere abweichende Fassung der Zeilen 6–7 findet sich lediglich in **SA**:
was der Mode Schwerd getheilt;
Bettler werden Fürstenbrüder,
während **SB**, **SC** und **SD** die revidierte Fassung überliefern:
was die Mode streng getheilt;
Alle Menschen werden Brüder,

2) **SA** und **SB** schreiben *siegen*; **SC** und **SD** *Siegen*

3) **SA**, **SB** und **SC** haben noch das altertümliche *Ahndest*, **SD** hat *Ahnest*.

Ein Vergleich mit den musikalischen Quellen von op. 125 zeigt, daß Beethoven wahrscheinlich **SD** oder einen Nachdruck davon als Textvorlage benutzt hat; dieser Text diente der vorliegenden Edition als Ausgangspunkt. In zwei kleinen Details, in denen Beethovens Schreibung in sich konsequent ist und auch **SA** entspricht, folgen dieser Quelle: *eine Seele* (**SB**, **SC**, **SD** *Eine Seele*), und nach *umschlungen* setzen wir kein Komma (dieses nur in **SD**).

Alle erreichbaren Versionen des Textes haben Gedankenstriche nach *Ja* und *Brüder*, doch ist ein solches Interpunktionszeichen für eine Musikedition nicht sonderlich geeignet, da es dort mit Silbentrennstrichen verwechselt werden könnte. Die vorliegende Edition folgt in der Setzung von Kommas und Ausrufungszeichen Quelle **E**. Ebenfalls aus **E** übernommen wurde die Interpunktion bei den einzelnen Ausrufen *Freude!* (T. 238, 240, 664 etc.) und in Textausschnitten, wie etwa in T. 767–781. Beethoven setzt in Quelle **A** innerhalb des einleitenden Rezitativs an nicht weniger als vier Stellen ein Ausrufungszeichen (T. 219, 221, 229, 236); wir haben das Ausrufungszeichen in T. 236 übernommen (da die Interpunktion in **X** durchgängig fehlt), folgen aber **C** und späteren Quellen in T. 219 und 229.

Veraltete Schreibungen wie *seyd*, *nent* und *getheilt* wurden stillschweigend modernisiert.

Bögen in Vokalstimmen

Beethovens Bögen in den Vokalstimmen fallen keinesfalls immer mit dem Silbenwechsel zusammen, sondern sind oftmals kürzer. Sie sind als echte Phrasierungsbögen und damit (anders als allgemein üblich) unabhängig von der

Textunterlegung zu sehen. Ein typisches Beispiel hierfür bieten T. 895–898. Auf der anderen Seite gibt es nur derartig wenige Beispiele für Bögen, die über die Silben hinausreichen, daß man sie getrost als Fehlschreibungen übergehen kann. Sie sind gewöhnlich dort anzutreffen, wo die Wörter nachträglich eingefügt zu sein scheinen; in der Tat sind solche überlangen Bögen nur in **A** anzutreffen und wurden vermutlich in **X** nicht übernommen. Es gibt jedoch eine Stelle, an der solch ein Bogen eine echte Bedeutung zu haben scheint und deshalb übernommen wurde (Sopran T. 840).

Dynamik in Vokalstimmen

Beethoven notiert in **A** dynamische Bezeichnungen oftmals nur im System des Sopran. Aus dem Kontext ist jedoch offenkundig, daß diese Dynamik generell für alle Stimmen intendiert ist, und er vergißt fast nie, diesbezügliche Auslassungen in **C** rückgängig zu machen (z.B. in T. 282). Wenn Beethoven dies trotzdem gelegentlich vergessen hat (z.B. in T. 280), so haben wir uns doch die Freiheit genommen, in diesen ganz offenkundigen Fällen ohne Kommentar zu ergänzen. Dies ist jedoch eindeutig nicht der Fall im Solo-Sopran T. 798–800. In Zweifelsfällen (wie T. 797 oder 742) folgt die Edition strikt den Quellen.

Richtbuchstaben

Um die vorliegende Ausgabe so bequem benutzbar wie nur möglich zu machen, wurden die traditionellen Richtbuchstaben übernommen, wie sie durchgehend in Aufführungs-Editionen von Beethovens Sinfonien enthalten sind. Es muß aber mit Nachdruck darauf hingewiesen werden, daß diese Buchstaben in keiner Weise authentisch, vielmehr erst einige Jahrzehnte nach Beethovens Tod eingeführt worden sind. Sie sind daher eher als eine äußere Beigabe denn als integraler Bestandteil der vorliegenden Edition anzusehen.

Dank

Es ist mir eine Freude, an dieser Stelle all die zu nennen, denen Dank zu sagen ist, als erste und vor allen Caroline Brown und Stephen Neiman von The Hanover Band, die den ersten Anstoß zu meinen Beethoven-Forschungen gaben und meine Arbeit über viele Jahre unterstützten. Die Mitarbeiter der Westminster Music Library, London, und David Royal von The London Borough of Lambeth Library Service waren unermüdlich hilfreich bei der Suche nach vielen Artikeln in ungezählten Zeitschriften; ich danke ihnen für ihre Geduld und Ausdauer. Dank gilt auch den Mitarbeitern der vielen Bibliotheken, an denen ich meine Forschungen durchführte: den beiden Häusern der Staatsbibliothek zu Berlin – Preußischer Kulturbesitz; dem Archiv der Gesellschaft der Musikfreunde in Wien; der British Library, London; der Library of the Royal College of Music, London; dem Stadtarchiv Aachen; und Schott Musik International, Mainz, dem ich ganz besonderen Dank schulde. Ergänzend dazu bin ich einer Reihe von Persönlichkeiten für Hilfe in der einen oder anderen Art im Verlauf meiner Forschungen zu Dank verpflichtet: Otto Biba, Sieghard Brandenburg, Nicholas Cook, Barry Cooper, William Drabkin, John Eliot Gardiner, Roy Goodman, Stephen Johnson, H. C. Robbins Landon, Sir Charles Mackerras, Graham Nattrass, Sir Simon Rattle, Nigel Simeone, Peter Stadlen und John Warrack.

Ein besonderer Dank gilt The British Academy, deren Unterstützung in der Endphase den Abschluß meiner Forschungsarbeit ermöglicht hat.

Schließlich danke ich ganz besonders meiner Mutter, Pauline Del Mar, und meiner Frau, Annabel Teh Gallop, für unendlich viel Hilfe und Geduld bei der Fertigstellung des Manuskripts zum Critical Commentary.

Jonathan Del Mar

(Deutsche Übersetzung: Dietrich Berke)

Sinfonie

mit Schlußchor über Schillers Ode „An die Freude",

für großes Orchester, 4 Solo und 4 Chorstimmen,

componirt und

Seiner Majestät dem König von Preußen

Friedrich Wilhelm III

in tiefster Ehrfurcht zugeeignet

von

Ludwig van Beethoven

125tes Werk.

(Eigenhändige Eintragung Beethovens auf dem Titelblatt des Widmungsexemplars, 1826 /
Beethoven's own inscription on the title-page of the dedication copy, 1826)

Symphonie Nr. 9

d-moll

op. 125

Ludwig van Beethoven

10
p cresc.
p cresc.
cresc.
cresc.
cresc.
cresc.
cresc.
cresc.
cresc.
cresc.
cresc.
cresc.
cresc.
cresc.
cresc.
ff

17
a 2
a 2
tr

A
27
f
p
sf
dimin.
a 2
6

36
pp cresc.
pp
cresc.
pp
cresc.
pp
cresc.
pp
cresc.
sotto voce
cresc.
pp
cresc.
pp
pp
cresc.
pp
cresc.
pp
pp
cresc.

47
cresc.
ff
tr

53
sf
Vc. e B.

61
B
sf
ben marcato
sf ben marcato
f
B
ben marcato

67
sf
f
a 2

73
p dolce
a 2
p

80
p
p
a 2
p
sempre piano
sempre piano
sempre piano
sempre piano

88
a 2
Vc.
B.
cresc.
p
f

C
a 2
cresc.
più cresc.

101
ff
p dolce
p
a 2
Vc. e B.

110
pp
sempre pp
Vc.
B.
pizz.
[pp]

117
pp
sempre pp
pp
pp
pp
pp
pp
sempre pp
sempre pp
sempre pp
pp
sempre pp
pp
sempre pp
6
pp
arco
pp

124
cresc.
Vc. e B.

130
D
cresc.
f
sf
a 2
D
non ligato
non ligato

134
sf
a 2
f
[sf]

138
p espressivo
p espressivo

144
p espressivo
Vc.
B.

150
E
E
Vc. e B.

158
dimin.
p
pp
a 2
6
Vc.
B.

168
pp
pp
pp
pp
pp
a 2
pp
pp
pp
pp

177
pp
a 2
pp
pp

184
espressivo
cresc.
[pp]
f
sf
a 2
ff

191
F
ritard. a tempo
p espressivo
[p]
a 2
F
ritard. a tempo
Vc. e B.

198
p
cresc.
a 2
Vc.
B.
pizz.

205
a 2
arco

G
210
ritard. a tempo
p
cresc.
p espress.
G
ritard. a tempo
Vc. e B.

217
f
sf
a 2

224
a 2
a 2
a 2
f

*) Autograph: 

236
H
sf
f
a 2
6

242
f
[f]
sf

248
f
f
[f]
[f]

253
I
p
più piano
più piano
p dimin.
dimin.
p
più piano
più piano
p
p
p
p
I
p
più piano
p
più piano
p
più piano
p
più piano

258
pp
cantabile
p
Vc.
B.

staccato
265
cresc.
pp
staccato
cresc.
staccato
cresc.
pp
[staccato]
cresc.
pp
[staccato]
cresc.
pp
[staccato]
cresc.
[staccato]
cresc.
pp
[staccato]
cresc.
pp
cresc.
cresc.
cresc.
cresc.
cresc.
pp
pizz.
cresc.

272
pp
a 2
a 2
pizz.

279
espressivo
a 2
a 2
a 2
un poco meno piano
un poco meno piano
un poco meno piano
Vc. e B.
arco

287
a 2
p
p
p
p
p
Vc.
B.

294
cresc.
f
II. p
a 2
[f
f]
sf

K
301
ff
K
Vc. e B.

310
ff
sf

316
ff
f
[ff]
sf

324
Vc.
B.
ben marcato

331

339
L
p dolce
p dolce
p
p
p
dolce
p
p dolce
p
p
p
p
L
p
p
p
Vc. e B.
p

347
espressivo
espressivo
espressivo
espressivo
p
p

354
cresc.
p
[p]
Vc.
B.

360
cresc.
f
sf
p cresc.
[p] cresc.

366
cresc.
cresc.

M
373
ff
p
pp
ten.
pizz.
[pp]

380
pp
sempre pp
pp
sempre pp
sempre pp
sempre pp
sempre pp
pp
sempre pp
sempre pp
sempre pp
sempre pp

386
pp
cresc.
sempre pp
cresc.
sempre pp
cresc.
sempre pp
cresc.
sempre pp
cresc.
pp
cresc.
pp
cresc.
pp
cresc.
pp
cresc.
pp
cresc.
arco
pp
cresc.

393
Vc. e B.

399
cresc.
f
sf
non ligato
Vc.
B.

403
[sf]
sf
[s]f
Vc. e B.
tr

N
407
p espressivo
p espressivo
p espressivo
N

414
Vc.
B.

420
Vc. e B.

427
O
p
Solo
espressivo
pizz.
6

435
cresc.
cresc.
cresc.
cresc.
cresc.
cresc.
cresc.
cresc.
cresc.
cresc.
cresc.
cresc.
cresc.

441
cresc.

448
P
cresc.
ff
P
Vc.
arco
B.
arco

454
p cresc.
cresc.
p

461
cresc.
f
sf
Vc. e B.

Q
469
p
sempre p
Solo dolce
II.
Solo
Q
sempre p

478
cresc.

485
cresc.
dimin.
cresc.
cresc.
dim.
cresc.
cresc.
cresc.
f
ff
dimin.

R
492
pp
cresc.
f
p
dimin.
più piano
R

498
cresc.
f
[p] cresc.
p cresc.

505
ritard. a tempo
ritard. a tempo
p espressivo
ritard. a tempo
ritard. a tempo

513
tr
p
pp
a 2
Vc.
B.

520
tr
p cresc.
cresc.
a 2

527
S
f più f
ff
sf

534
sempre ff
ff
tr

541
sf
ff
tr

Molto vivace 𝅗𝅥. = 116
Flauto I
Flauto II
Oboe I
Oboe II
Clarinetto I in Do / C
Clarinetto II in Do / C
Fagotto I
Fagotto II
Corno I, II in Re / D
Corno III, IV in Si♭ / B basso
Clarino I, II in Re / D
Trombone I Alto
Trombone II Tenore
Trombone III Basso
Timpani in
Molto vivace 𝅗𝅥. = 116
Violini I
Violini II
Viole
Violoncelli e Bassi
ff
sf
pp

13
sempre pp
pp
sempre pp
sempre pp
sempre pp
pp
Vc.
B.

26
I
Fl.
II
pp
I
Ob.
II
pp
I
Clar.
II
I
Fag.
II
I
II
Cor.
III
IV
pp
sempre pp
Clno. I
II
Timp.
I
Viol.
II
Vle.
Vc.
B.
sempre pp
sempre pp
sempre pp
sempre pp
sempre pp

39
cresc.
sempre pp
sempre pp

A
53
ff
f
A
ff
f

67
B
B

81
C
cresc.
p cresc.
ff
a 2
C
cresc.
p cresc.
ff
Vc. e B.
pizz.
[p] cresc.
arco

94
a 2
a 2

107
D
p
a 2
a 2
a 2
a 2
D
p

120
p cresc.
f
a 2

133
f
pp
sempre pp
a 2
II. pp
Vc.
B.

145
pp
pp
pp
pp
pp
pp
pp
pp
pp
pp
sempre pp
sempre pp
sempre pp
Vc. e B.
sempre pp

159
cresc.

171
"Ritmo di tre battute"
"Ritmo di tre battute"
sempre p
sempre p
"Ritmo di tre battute"
pizz.
[p]
pizz.
[p]
pizz.
[p]
pizz.
[p]

183
"Ritmo di tre battute"
p
sempre p
sempre p
sempre p
sempre p
"Ritmo
f

196
E
p
dimin.
di tre battute"
E

209
pp
dimin.
p
Vc.
B.
arco
pizz.
p dimin.
dimin.

222
"Ritmo di tre battute"
sempre pp
sempre pp
sempre pp
sempre pp
sempre pp
pp
pp
"Ritmo di tre battute"
pp
sempre pp
pp
arco
pp
sempre pp
pizz.
arco
pp
sempre pp
pizz.
arco
pp
sempre pp
pizz.
Vc. e B.
[pp]

"Ritmo di quattro battute"
234
pp
sempre pp
"Ritmo di quattro battute"
pp
sempre pp
pp
sempre pp
pp
sempre pp
"Ritmo di quattro battute"
pp
a 2
p [p]
"Ritmo di quattro battute"
arco
pp
sempre pp
arco
pp
sempre pp
arco
pp
sempre pp
Vc.
arco
pp
sempre pp
B.
arco
pp
sempre pp
"Ritmo di quattro battute"

F
245
pp
sempre pp
a 2
F
sempre pp

256
cresc.
più cresc.
f più f
a 2
Vc. e B.
f
più f

G
268
ff
a 2
3
G

280
a 2
a 2
a 2

H
292
a 2
a 2
p cresc.
cresc.
H
pizz.
[p]

304
p
cresc.
dimin.
p cresc.
Vc.
arco
B.
pizz.

317
p cresc.
cresc.
p cresc.
cresc.
p cresc.
p cresc.
cresc.
cresc.
cresc.
p cresc.
pizz.
cresc.
pizz.
cresc.
pizz.
cresc.
cresc.
cresc.

I
330
ff
ff
ff
ff
ff
ff
ff
ff
ff
ff
ff
[ff]
I arco
ff
arco
sim.
ff
arco
ff
ff
arco
ff

342
a 2
a 2
Vc. e B.

K
354
p
cresc.
f
K

376
pp
sempre pp

388
1.
pp
sempre pp
1.

388b
2.
cresc.
ff
pp
[f]
f
sempre pp
p cresc.
2.

stringendo il tempo
400
pp
cresc.
stringendo il tempo

*) Cf. / Vgl. Critical Commentary.

422
1.
2.
cresc.
p
p cresc.
Vc.
B.

430
L
p cresc.
p
cresc.
dolce
cresc.
fp
L
p staccato
cresc.
p

441
p
p
p
p
p
p

453
Vc. e B.

464
cresc.
p
cresc.
p
cresc.
cresc.
cresc.
p
cresc.
cresc.
p
cresc.
cresc.
p
cresc.

M
475
fp
cresc.
f
M
fp
cresc.
f

486
1.
2.
p
sempre staccato
cresc.
fp
Vc.
B.

497
f
dimin.
p
cresc.
a 2

509
cresc.
f
dimin.
[f]

poco ritard.
520
sempre più piano
pp
sempre pp
poco ritard.

531
Molto vivace
Fl.
I
II
Ob.
I
II
Clar.
I
II
Fag.
I
II
Cor.
I
II
III
IV
Clno.
I
II
Timp.
Molto vivace
Viol.
I
II
Vle.
Vc. e B.
ff
sf
pp

543
sempre pp
pp
Vc.
B.

556
pp
pp
pp
sempre pp
sempre pp
sempre pp
sempre pp
sempre pp
sempre pp

569
cresc.
sempre pp

583
N
N

597
O
O

611
cresc.
ff
p cresc.
a 2
Vc. e B.
pizz.
[p] cresc.
arco

624
a 2
a 2

637
a 2
a 2
a 2
a 2
p

650
P
p cresc.
f
a 2
P
p cresc.
f

663
f
pp
sempre pp
a 2
II. pp
Vc.
B.

675
pp
pp
pp
pp
pp
pp
pp
pp
pp
pp
sempre pp
sempre pp
sempre pp
Vc. e B.
sempre pp

689
cresc.

701
"Ritmo di tre battute"
"Ritmo di tre battute"
sempre p
sempre p
"Ritmo di tre battute"
pizz.
[p]
pizz.
[p]
pizz.
[p]
pizz.
[p]

713
"Ritmo di tre battute"
p
sempre p
sempre p
sempre p
sempre p

725
Q
p
dimin.
"Ritmo di tre battute"
f
Q

739
pp
dimin.
p
pp
arco
pizz.
p dimin.
Vc.
B.
dimin.

752
"Ritmo di tre battute"
sempre pp
pp
"Ritmo di tre battute"
arco
pizz.
Vc. e B.
[pp]

"Ritmo di quattro battute"
764
pp
sempre pp
"Ritmo di quattro battute"
pp
sempre pp
pp
sempre pp
pp
sempre pp
"Ritmo di quattro battute"
pp
a 2
p[p]
"Ritmo di quattro battute"
arco
pp
sempre pp
arco
pp
sempre pp
arco
pp
sempre pp
Vc.
arco
pp
sempre pp
B.
arco
pp
sempre pp
"Ritmo di quattro battute"

R
775
pp
sempre pp
a 2
R
sempre pp

786
cresc.
più cresc.
f più f
a 2
più f
Vc. e B.

S
798
ff
a 2
3
S

810
a 2
a 2
a 2
f

822
T
a 2
a 2
p cresc.
cresc.
pizz.
[p]

834
p
cresc.
dimin.
p cresc.
Vc.
B.
arco
pizz.

847
p cresc.
cresc.
p cresc.
cresc.
p cresc.
p cresc.
cresc.
cresc.
cresc.
p cresc.
pizz.
cresc.
pizz.
cresc.
pizz.
cresc.
cresc.
cresc.

U
860
ff
[ff]
U arco
arco
0
sim.

872
a 2
a 2
Vc. e B.

884
V
p
cresc.
f
V

895

906
pp
sempre pp

918
Coda
Fl.
Ob.
Clar.
Fag.
Cor.
Clno.
Trb. III
Timp.
Viol.
Vle.
Vc. e B.
cresc.
p cresc.
[f]
sempre pp

stringendo il tempo
Presto
931
pp
cresc.
ff
f
stringendo il tempo
Presto

944
fp
ff
f
p
Vc.
B.

Adagio molto e cantabile ♩ = 60
Flauto I
Flauto II
Oboe I
Oboe II
Clarinetto I in Si♭ / B
Clarinetto II in Si♭ / B
Fagotto I
Fagotto II
Corno I, II in Si♭ / B basso
Corno III, IV in Mi♭ / Es
Clarino I, II in Si♭ / B
Timpani in Si♭/B - Fa/F
Adagio molto e cantabile ♩ = 60
Violini I
mezza voce
Violini II
Viole
Violoncelli
Bassi

10
dolce
dolce
dolce
dolce
dolce
*)
dolce
cresc.
cresc.
cresc.
cresc.
cresc.
p
p
p
p

*) Autograph:

19
cresc.
p
più piano
pp
più p.
[p]

25
Andante moderato ♩ = 63
p
cresc.
Andante moderato ♩ = 63
espressivo
cresc.
espressivo
cresc.
p cresc.

32
cresc.
p
morendo
p cresc.
cresc.
pizz.

*) Cf. / Vgl. Critical Commentary.

45
sempre staccato
sempre staccato
dolce
arco
pizz.

50

*) Autograph: 

60
pp
cresc.
p
più piano
pp
più p
Vc. e B.

Andante moderato
65
cresc.
p cresc.
pp
morendo
Andante moderato
Vc.
B.

73
cresc.
p
morendo
a 2
pizz.

81
Tempo I
più p - - pp
più p - - pp
più piano - - pp
dolce
più piano - - pp
dolce
più piano - - pp
dolce
più piano - - pp
a 2
più piano - - pp
dolce
Tempo I
pizz.
più piano - pp
pizz.
più piano - pp
pizz.
più piano - pp
pizz.
più piano - - pp
più p - - pp

88
p

94
p
cresc.

Stesso tempo
99
p dolce
p dolce
p dolce
p
p dolce
p dolce
p dolce
p
p
p
p
sempre p
Stesso tempo
arco
p dolce
pizz.
[p]
pizz.
[p]
Vc. e B. pizz.
[p]

102
cresc.
p
cresc.
p
p
p
cresc.
p
cresc.
dimin.
p

105

108
cresc.
p
cresc.
cresc.
cresc.

111
cresc.
tr
9

113
p
dimin.

115
cresc.
p
dimin.

119
più piano
pp
cresc.
f
sf
ff
III.
[più piano
cresc.]
arco

123
A
dolce
dolce
dolce
dolce
p dolce
dolce
A espressivo
dolce
pizz.
[p]
pizz.
[p]
pizz.
[p]

127
cantabile
cresc. poco a poco
cantabile
cresc. poco a poco
cresc. poco a poco
cresc. poco a poco
cresc. poco a poco
cresc. poco a poco
cresc. poco a poco
a 2
cresc. poco a poco
arco
cresc. poco a poco
arco
cresc. poco a poco
Vc.
arco
cresc. poco a poco
B.
arco
cresc. poco a poco

130
Vc. e B.

B
133
p
pp
cresc.
p dolce
pizz.
unis.

138
cresc.
p
dolce
cresc.
p
dolce
cresc.
p
dolce
cresc.
p
dolce
cresc.
p
cresc.
p
p
cresc.
dolce cantabile
arco
cresc.
arco
cresc.
arco
cresc.

141
cresc.
cresc.
cresc.
[cresc.]
cresc.
cresc.
cresc.
pizz.
cresc.
pizz.
cresc.
pizz.
cresc.

144
cresc.
p
9

146
cresc.
ff
dimin.
p
pp
f
arco
9

149
C
cresc.
f
p
sempre
sempre dimin.
C
pizz.

152
pp
cresc.
dimin.
sempre pp
arco
[dimin.
]

155
f
f
p
f
pp
pizz.
[pp]
fp

Presto 𝅗𝅥. = 66
Flauto piccolo
Flauto I
Flauto II
Oboe I
Oboe II
Clarinetto I in Si♭/B
Clarinetto II in Si♭/B
Fagotto I
Fagotto II
Contrafagotto
Corno I, II in Re/D
Corno III, IV in Si♭/B basso
Clarino I, II in Re/D
I Alto
Trombone II Tenore
III Basso
Timpani in Re/D - La/A
Triangolo, Cinelli e Gran Tamburo
SOLI
Soprano
Alto
Tenore
Baritono
CORO
Soprani
Alti
Tenori
Bassi
Presto 𝅗𝅥. = 66
Violini I
Violini II
Viole
Violoncelli e Bassi
ff

*) Autograph: no tie / kein Haltebogen.

17
ff
f

*) Autograph: [musical example] (?); Cf. / Vgl. Critical Commentary.

Tempo I
Tempo I

40
ritard.
poco adagio
in Si♭/B
in Re/D
in Si♭/B
in Re/D
ritard.
poco adagio
Vc. e B.
dimin.

Vivace
48
Tempo I
Vivace
pizz.
Tempo I
pizz.
pizz.
pizz.
Vc.
arco
B.

Adagio cantabile
Tempo I
58
[dolce]
dolce
p
in Si♭/B
dolce
[p]
dolce
p
in Re/D
in Si♭/B
p
in Re/D
Adagio cantabile
Tempo I
Vc. e B.
dimin.
p

67
p
cresc.
p
cresc.
p
cresc.
p
p
p
p
p
cresc.
ff

77
Allegro assai 𝅗𝅥 = 80
Tempo I
dolce
in Si♭/B
in Re/D
in Si♭/B
in Re/D
Allegro assai 𝅗𝅥 = 80
Tempo I

85
in La/A
in La/A

92
Allegro assai 𝅗𝅥 = 80
Clarinetti in La / A
in Re/D
in Si♭/B
in Re/D
Allegro assai 𝅗𝅥 = 80
p

102
cresc.
p
cresc.

112
in La/A
p
sempre piano
in Re/D
in Si♭/B
in Re/D
[arco]
p
sempre piano
Vc.
p
sempre piano
B.
p
sempre piano

122
p
cresc.
p
cresc.
p
cresc.
p
cresc.
p
cresc.
p

131
in La/A
cresc. p
cresc. p
in Re/D
in Si♭/B
in Re/D
[arco]
p
cresc. p
cresc. p
cresc. p

140
A
A
[arco]
p dolce

149
in La/A
cresc.
p
in Re/D
in Si♭/B
in Re/D

156
cresc.
cresc.
cresc.
cresc.
cresc.
cresc.
cresc.
cresc.

B
164
in La/A
in Re/D
in Si♭/B
in Re/D
B
Vc. e B.

171

178
sf
in La/A
in Re/D
in Si♭/B
in Re/D

C
185
C
non ligato
non ligato

191
in La/A
in Re/D
in Si♭/B
in Re/D
sempre f
sempre f
sempre f
sempre f

195

199
in La/A
in Re/D
in Si♭/B
in Re/D
sf
3

poco ritenente
poco adagio
Tempo I
203
p
f
[p]
cresc. f
cresc. f
[cresc.] f
[f]
poco ritenente
poco adagio
Tempo I
Vc.
B.
[p] f

Presto
208
Fl. I II
Ob. I II
Clar. I II
in La/A
Fag. I II
Cfg.
Cor. I II
in Re/D
III IV
in Si♭/B
Clno. I II
in Re/D
Timp.
Recitativo
Bar. Solo
Presto
Viol. I II
Vle.
Vc. e B.
ff

*) Execution / Ausführung: [musical example] Tö-ne! ; cf. / Vgl. Critical Commentary

228
in La/A
in Re/D
in Si♭/B
in Re/D
ad libitum
neh-me-re an-stim-men, und freu - - - - - - den-vol-le-re!

237
Allegro assai
Fl. I II
Ob. I II
p dolce
pp
Clar. I II
dolce
pp
Fag. I II
dolce
Cfg.
Cor. I II
p
III IV
Clno. I II
Timp.
SOLI
Sop.
Alt.
Ten.
Bar.
f
(angenehm)
Freu - de,
Freu - de__, Freu - de, schö - ner Göt - ter - fun - ken,
CORO
Sop.
Alt.
Ten.
Bass.
f
Freu - de!
Freu - de!
Allegro assai
Viol. I II
pizz.
p
Vle.
Vc. e B.

243
in La/A
in Re/D
in Si♭/B
in Re/D
Tochter aus E - ly - si-um, Wir be - tre-ten feu-er - trun-ken, Himm-li - sche, dein Hei - lig-tum. Dei-ne Zau-ber

250
cresc.
p
a 2
bin - den wieder, Was die Mode streng ge - teilt; Al - le Menschen wer-den Brü-der, Wo dein sanf - ter Flü - gel weilt.

D
257
in La/A
a 2
in Re/D
in Si♭/B
in Re/D
f
Dei - ne Zau - ber bin - den wie - der, Was die Mo - de streng ge - teilt; Al - le Men - schen wer - den Brü - der,
Dei - ne Zau - ber bin - den wie - der, Was die Mo - de streng ge - teilt; Al - le Men - schen wer - den Brü - der,
Dei ne Zau ber bin den wie der, Was die Mo de streng ge teilt; Al le Men schen wer den Brü der,
D
arco
arco
arco
arco

263
sempre f
sempre f
sempre f
a 2
sempre f
p dolce
Wo dein sanf - ter Flü - gel weilt.
Wo dein sanf - ter Flü - gel weilt.
Wo dein sanf - ter Flü - gel weilt.
sempre f
sempre f
sempre f
sempre f

269
p dolce
in La/A
p dolce
in Re/D
in Si♭/B
in Re/D
Wer ein holdes Weib er - run - gen, Mische sei-nen
Wem der gro-ße Wurf ge - lun - gen, Ei-nes Freundes Freund zu sein, Wer ein holdes Weib er - run - gen, Mische sei-nen
Wem der gro-ße Wurf ge - lun - gen, Ei-nes Freundes Freund zu sein, Wer ein holdes Weib er - run - gen, Mische sei-nen
Wem der gro-ße Wurf ge - lun - gen, Ei-nes Freundes Freund zu sein, Wer ein holdes Weib er - run - gen, Mische sei-nen
Vc.
p
B.

276
cresc.
cresc.
cresc.
dimin.
cresc.
sf
dimin.
Ju - bel ein! Ja, wer auch nur ei - ne _ See - le Sein nennt auf dem Er - den - rund! Und _ wer's nie ge - konnt, der steh - le
Ju - bel ein ___! Ja, wer auch nur ei - ne See - le _ Sein nennt auf dem Er - den - rund! Und _ wer's nie ge - konnt, der steh - le
Ju - bel ein ___! Ja, wer auch nur ei - ne _ See - le _ Sein nennt auf dem Er - den - rund! Und _ wer's nie ge - konnt, der steh - le
Ju - bel ein! Ja ___, wer auch nur ei - ne _ See - le Sein nennt auf dem Er - den - rund! Und _ wer's nie ge - konnt, der steh - le _
cresc.
dimin.

283
E
a 2
in La/A
in Re/D
in Si♭/B
in Re/D
Weinend sich aus die - sem Bund!
Weinend sich aus die - sem Bund!
Weinend sich aus die - sem Bund!
Weinend sich aus die- sem Bund!
Ja, wer auch nur ei - ne _ See - le Sein nennt auf dem Er - den - rund! Und _ wer's nie ge -
Ja, wer auch nur ei - ne See - le _ Sein nennt auf dem Er - den - rund! Und _ wer's nie ge -
Ja, wer auch nur ei - ne _ See - le _ Sein nennt auf dem Er - den - rund! Und _ wer's nie ge -
Ja ___ , wer auch nur ei - ne See - le Sein nennt auf dem Er - den - rund! Und _ wer's nie ge -
cresc.
poco cresc.

290
a 2
dimin.
p
sempre piano
sempre p
pp
Vc. e B.
Freu -
Freu -
konnt, der steh - le Wei - nend sich aus die - sem Bund!
konnt, der steh - le Wei - nend sich aus die - sem Bund!
konnt, der steh - le Wei - nend sich aus die - sem Bund!
konnt, der steh - le Wei - nend sich aus die - sem Bund!

297
F
in La/A
p
in Re/D
in Si♭/B
in Re/D
Al - - le_ Gu-ten, al-le_ Bö-sen
- de trin-ken al-le_ We-sen An den Brü-sten der Na-tur; Al-le Gu-ten, al-le Bö-sen
- de trin-ken al-le_ We-sen An den Brü-sten der Na-tur; Al-le Gu-ten, al-le Bö-sen
F
sempre piano
sempre piano
Vc.
sempre piano
B.

p sempre piano
sempre p
303
Küs - - se_ gab sie uns und Re - ben, Ei - nen Freund, ge - prüft im_ Tod; Wol -
Fol-gen ih - rer Ro - sen - spur. Küs - se gab sie uns und Re - ben, Ei - nen Freund, ge - prüft im Tod; Wol -
Fol-gen ih - rer Ro - sen - spur. Küs - se_ gab sie uns und Re - ben, Ei - nen Freund, ge - prüft im_ Tod; Wol -
Fol-gen ih - rer Ro - sen - spur. Küs - se gab sie uns und Re - ben, Ei - nen Freund, ge - prüft im_ Tod; Wol -
sempre piano

309
G
in La/A
in Re/D
in Si♭/B
in Re/D
cresc.
f
lust ward dem Wurm ge - ge - ben, Und der Che-rub steht vor Gott.
lust ward dem Wurm ge - ge - ben, Und der Che-rub steht vor Gott.
lust ward dem Wurm ge - ge - ben, Und der Che-rub steht vor Gott.
lust ward dem Wurm ge - ge - ben, Und der Che-rub steht vor Gott.
Küs - se gab sie uns und Re - ben,
Küs - se gab sie uns und Re - ben,
Küs - se gab sie uns und Re - ben,
Küs - se gab sie uns und Re - ben,
tr
sempre f

315
I.
II.
ff
sf
Ei - nen Freund, ge - prüft im Tod; Wol - lust ward dem Wurm ge - ge - ben, Und der Che - rub
Ei - nen Freund, ge - prüft im Tod; Wol - lust ward dem Wurm ge - ge - ben, Und der Che - rub
Ei - nen Freund, ge - prüft im Tod; Wol - lust ward dem Wurm ge - ge - ben, Und der Che - rub
Ei - nen Freund, ge - prüft im Tod; Wol - lust ward dem Wurm ge - ge - ben, Und der Che - rub
sempre più f
tr

320
a 2
a 2
in La/A
Clarinetti in Si♭/B
a 2
ben marcato
sf
in Re/D
II. [ff]
in Si♭/B
in Re/D
steht vor Gott, und der Che - rub steht vor Gott, steht vor
steht vor Gott, und der Che - rub steht vor Gott, steht vor
sf
steht vor Gott, und der Che - rub steht vor Gott, steht vor
steht vor Gott, und der Che - rub steht vor Gott, steht vor
ben marcato
ben marcato
ben marcato
Vc. e B.
ben marcato
sf

326
ff
a 2
Corni in Si♭/B
molto tenuto
tr
Gott,
vor
Gott,
vor
Gott.
molto tenuto
tenuto

Allegro assai vivace [♩.] = 84
alla Marcia
331
Fl. picc.
Fl. I II
Ob. I II
Clar. I II in Si♭/B
Fag. I II
Cfg.
Cor. I in Re/D II
Cor. III in Si♭/B IV
Clno. I in Re/D
Clno. II in Si♭/B
Timp.
Trgl.
Cin.
Gr. Tamb.
Ten. Solo
Ten. I
Ten. II
CORO
Bass.
Allegro assai vivace [♩.] = 84
alla Marcia
Viol. I
II
Vle.
Vc. e B.
pp

340
pp
pp
pp
pp
pp
pp
Clarino II in Si♭/B
pp sempre pp
pp
pp
pp

349
in Si♭/B
in Re/D
in Si♭/B
II.
in Si♭/B

358
H
sempre pp
sempre pp
sempre pp
sempre pp
sempre pp
sempre pp
II.
sempre pp
sempre pp
sempre pp
H
pp
pp
pp
Vc.
pp
B.

367
in Si♭/B
in Re/D
in Si♭/B
in Si♭/B
II.
pp
Solo
Froh,

376
sempre pp
poco cresc.
II.
pp
froh, wie sei-ne Son-nen, sei-ne Son-nen flie-gen_, froh, wie sei-ne
Vc. e B.

385
I
in Si♭/B
in Re/D
in Si♭/B
II.
in Si♭/B
Son - nen flie - gen, Durch des Him - mels prächt' - gen Plan, Lau - fet, Brü - der, eu - re
I
poco cresc.
poco cresc.
poco cresc.
Vc.
poco cresc.
B.

394
poco f
II.
Bahn, lau - fet, Brü - der, eu - re Bahn, Freu - dig wie ein Held zum
Vc. e B.

402
in Si♭/B
in Re/D
in Si♭/B
II.
in Si♭/B
Sie - gen, wie ein Held zum Sie - gen, Lau - fet, Brü - der, eu - re Bahn
poco f
poco f
poco f
Vc.
poco f
B.

411
più f
II.
Lau - fet, Brü - der, eu - re Bahn, Freu - dig wie ein Held zum Sie - gen,
Lau - fet, Brü - der, eu - re Bahn, Freu - dig wie ein Held zum Sie - gen,
Lau - fet, Brü - der, eu - re Bahn, Freu - dig wie ein Held zum Sie - gen,
Vc. e B.

419
in Si♭/B
in Re/D
in Si♭/B
in Si♭/B
II.
f
più f
ff
sf
(N.B. Diese 6
wie ein Held zum Sie - - - gen, freu - dig,
wie ein Held zum Sie - gen, freu - dig, freu - dig
wie ein Held zum Sie - gen, freu - dig, freu - dig
wie ein Held zum Sie - gen, freu - dig, freu - dig

427
K
sempre l'istesso tempo
a 2
sempre ff
sf
a 2
sempre ff
a 2
sf
sempre ff
sf
II.
Clarino II in Re/D
Takte können nicht vom Chor, wohl aber von dem Solosänger ausgelassen werden.)
freu - dig wie ein Held, ein Held zum Sie - gen.
sf
wie ein Held zum Sie - - - - - gen.
sf
wie ein Held zum Sie - - - - - gen.
sf
wie ein Held zum Sie - - - - - gen.
K
sempre l'istesso tempo
sempre ff
sf
sf
sempre ff

434
a 2
in Si♭/B
a 2
sf
sf
in Re/D
ff
a 2
in Si♭/B
sf
sf
in Re/D
sempre ff
sf
sf

441
a 2
sf
sempre ff
a 2
sf
sempre ff
a 2
a 2
sf
sf
sf
sempre ff
sf
Vc.
sf
sf
B.

448
a 2
a 2
in Si♭/B
a 2
a 2
in Re/D
a 2
in Si♭/B
in Re/D
sf
sf
f
[ff]

455
a 2
sf
f
a 2
Vc. e B.
[sf]

463
in Si♭/B
in Re/D
in Si♭/B
in Re/D
sf

471

478
in Si♭/B
in Re/D
in Si♭/B
in Re/D

486
a 2
sf
Corni in Re/D

493
L
a 2
in Si♭/B
in Re/D
in Re/D
in Re/D
sf
L
[sf]

500
a 2

507
in Si♭/B
in Re/D
in Re/D
in Re/D

514
f
ff
sf

522
in Si♭/B
Clarinetti in La/A
in Re/D
in Re/D
in Re/D
sf
f
dimin.
p
più p

532
pp
pp cresc.
pp
pp
sempre pp
pp cresc.
pp
pp cresc.
pp
pp cresc.
pp
pp cresc.
pp
pp cresc.

M
543
Fl. I II
Ob. I II
in La/A
Clar. I II
Fag. I II
in Re/D
Cor. I II III IV
Clno. I II
Timp.
CORO
Sop.
Alt.
Ten.
Bass.
Freu - de, schö - ner Göt - ter - fun - ken, Toch - ter aus E - ly - si - um,
Freu - de, schö - ner Göt - ter - fun - ken, Toch - ter aus E - ly - si - um,
Freu - de, schö - ner Göt - ter - fun - ken, Toch - ter aus E - ly - si - um,
Freu - de, schö - ner Göt - ter - fun - ken, Toch - ter aus E - ly - si - um,
Viol. I II
Vle.
Vc. e B.
ff
f
sf

551
sf
Wir be - tre - ten feu - er - trun - ken, Himm - li - sche, dein Hei - lig - tum.
Wir be - tre - ten feu - er - trun - ken, Himm - li - sche, dein Hei - lig - tum.
Wir be - tre - ten feu - er - trun - ken, Himm - li - sche, dein Hei - lig - tum.
Wir be - tre - ten feu - er - trun - ken, Himm - li - sche, dein Hei - lig - tum.

559
in La/A
in Re/D
in Re/D
in Re/D
Dei - ne Zau - ber bin - den wie - der, Was die Mo - de streng ge - teilt; Al -
Dei - ne Zau - ber bin - den wie - der, Was die Mo - de streng ge - teilt; Al -
Dei - ne Zau - ber bin - den wie - der, Was die Mo - de streng ge - teilt; Al -
Dei - ne Zau - ber bin - den wie - der, Was die Mo - de streng ge - teilt; Al -
ff

567
sf
- - le Men - schen wer - den Brü - der, Wo dein sanf - ter Flü - gel
sf
- - le Men - schen wer - den Brü - der, Wo dein sanf - ter Flü - gel
sf
- - le Men - schen_ wer - den Brü - der, Wo dein sanf - ter Flü - gel
sf
- - le Men - schen wer - den Brü - der, Wo dein sanf - ter Flü - gel

574
in La/A
in Re/D
in Re/D
in Re/D
weilt. Dei - ne Zau - ber bin - den wie - der, Was die Mo - de
weilt. Dei - ne Zau - ber bin - den wie - der, Was die Mo - de
weilt. Dei - ne Zau - ber bin - den wie - der, Was die Mo - de
weilt. Dei - ne Zau - ber bin - den wie - der, Was die Mo - de

581
ff
sf
streng ge - teilt; Al - - - le Men - schen wer - den Brü - der, Wo dein
ff
sf
streng ge - teilt; Al - - - le Men - schen wer - den Brü - der, Wo dein
ff
sf
streng ge - teilt; Al - - - le Men - schen wer - den Brü - der, Wo dein
ff
sf
streng ge - teilt; Al - - - le Men - schen wer - den Brü - der, Wo dein
ff
ff
ff
ff

588
in La/A
in Re/D
in Re/D
in Re/D
sf
[sf]
sanf - ter Flü - gel weilt.
sanf - ter Flü - gel weilt.
sanf - ter Flü - gel weilt.
sanf - ter Flü - gel weilt.

Andante maestoso 𝅗𝅥 = 72
595
Fl. I II
Ob. I II
Clar. I II in La/A
Fag. I II
Cfg.
Cor. I II
Trb. I II III
Timp.
CORO
Sop.
Alt.
Ten.
Bass.
Seid um - schlungen Mil - li - o - nen! Die - sen Kuß der gan - zen Welt!
Seid um - schlungen Mil - li - o - nen! Die - sen Kuß der gan - zen Welt!
Andante maestoso 𝅗𝅥 = 72
Viol. I II
Vle.
Vc. e B.

603
in La/A
in Re/D
f Seid um - schlun - gen Mil - - - - - li - o - nen! sf Die - - - sen
f Seid um - schlun - gen Mil - - - - - li - o - nen! Die - - - - sen
f Seid um - schlun - gen Mil - - - - li - o - nen! sf Die - sen
f Seid um - schlun - gen Mil - - - - - li - o - nen! sf Die - - - sen

608
N
Kuß der gan - - - zen Welt!
Kuß der gan - - - zen Welt!
Kuß der gan - - - zen Welt! Brü - der! ü - berm Ster - nen - zelt Muß ein
Kuß der gan - - - zen Welt! Brü - der! ü - berm Ster - nen - zelt Muß ein
N

616
in La/A
in Re/D
a 2
Brü - - der! ü - berm Ster - - nen -
lie - ber Va - ter woh - nen.
Brü - - der! ü - - berm Ster - - nen -

622
a 2
a 2
zelt Muß ein lie - - ber Va - - ter woh - nen.
zelt Muß ein lie - - ber Va - - ter woh - nen.
zelt Muß ein lie - - ber Va - - ter woh - nen.
zelt Muß ein lie - - ber Va - - ter woh - nen.
Vle. I.
Vle. II.
Vc.
B.

Adagio ma non troppo ma divoto 𝅗𝅥 = 60
627
a 2
in La/A
in Re/D
cresc.
p
pp
Ihr stürzt nie - der, Mil - li - o - nen?
Adagio ma non troppo ma divoto 𝅗𝅥 = 60

635
a 2
cresc.
ff
p
pp
f
Ah - nest du den Schöpfer, Welt? Such' ihn ü - berm Ster - nen - zelt!
Ah - nest du den Schöpfer, Welt? Such' ihn ü - berm Ster - nen - zelt!
Ah - nest du den Schöpfer, Welt? Such' ihn ü - berm Ster - nen - zelt!
Ah - nest du den Schöpfer, Welt? Such' ihn ü - berm Ster - nen - zelt!

643
in La/A
in Re/D
Ü - ber Ster - nen muß er woh - nen,
Ü - ber Ster - nen muß er woh - nen,
Ü - ber Ster - nen muß er woh - nen,
Ü - ber Ster - nen muß er woh - nen,

650
pp
sempre pp
ü - - ber Ster - nen muß er woh - - - - - nen.
ü - - ber Ster - nen muß er woh - - - - - nen.
ü - ber Ster - nen muß er woh - nen.
ü - ber Ster - nen muß er woh - nen.
Vc. e B.

Allegro energico e sempre ben marcato 𝅗𝅥. = 84
655
Fl. I II
Ob. I II
a 2
Clar. I II in La/A
Fag. I II
Cfg.
Cor. I II in Re/D
III IV
Clno. I II in Re/D
Trb. I II III
Timp.
CORO
Sop.
Freu - de, schö - ner Göt - ter - fun - ken, Toch - ter aus E - ly - si - um,
Alt.
Seid um - schlun - gen Mil - li - o - nen!
Ten.
Bass.
Allegro energico e sempre ben marcato 𝅗𝅥. = 84
Viol. I II
Vle.
Vc. e B.

659
a 2
a 2
a 2
a 2
Wir be - tre - ten feu - er - trun - ken, Himm - li - sche, dein Hei - lig - tum.
Die - sen Kuß der gan - zen Welt! Seid
Seid
Vc.
B.

663
a 2
in La/A
in Re/D
in Re/D
I.
Freu - de! Freu - de! Wir be -
um - schlun - gen Mil - li - o - nen! Die - sen
um - schlun - gen Mil - li - o - nen! Die - sen
Freu - de, schö - ner Göt - ter - fun - ken, Toch - ter aus E - ly - si - um, Wir be - tre - ten

668
O
a 2
tre - ten dein Hei -
Kuß der gan - zen Welt! Freu - de!
Kuß der gan - zen Welt! Freu - de, schö - ner Göt - ter - fun - ken,
feu - er - trun - ken, Himm - li - sche, dein Hei - lig - tum. Seid um - schlun - gen

673
a 2
a 2
a 2
in La/A
a 2
in Re/D
in Re/D
- - - - - - - - - - - - lig - tum ________ .
Freu - de! Wir be - tre - ten_dein ____ Hei - - lig -
Toch - ter aus E - ly - si - um ____ , Wir be - tre - ten feu - er - trun - ken, Himm - li - sche, dein
Mil - li - - o - nen! Die - sen Kuß der gan - zen
sf

678
a 2
a 2
a 2
Seid um - schlun - gen Mil - li - - o - nen!
tum. Freu - de, schö - ner Göt - ter-fun - ken, Toch - ter aus E - ly - si - um,
Hei - lig-tum. Freu - de! Freu - de!
Welt

683
a 2
a 2
a 2
in La/A
a 2
II. [f] II. [f]
f f f f
in Re/D
in Re/D
sf sf
sf
Die - sen Kuß der gan - zen Welt, die - sen
Wir be - tre - ten feu - er - trun - ken, Himm - li - sche, dein Hei - lig - tum, dein
Wir be - tre - ten dein Hei - - - - - - - -
, die - sen Kuß der gan - zen
f
Vc. e B.
f f f f

688
a 2
a 2
a 2
a 2
Kuß der gan - zen Welt, der gan - zen Welt!
Hei - - - - - - - lig - tum.
ff
Seid
- lig - tum, dein Hei - - - - - - - - -
Welt, die - sen Kuß der gan - zen Welt!
Vc.
B.

P
a 2
693
in La/A
in Re/D
in Re/D
Freu - de, schö - ner Göt - ter-fun - ken, Wir be-tre - ten feu - er-trun - ken, Himm - li-sche, dein
um - schlun - gen Mil - li - o - nen! Die - sen
lig -
Freu - de! Freu - de! Wir be -
P

698
a 2
a 2
a 2
a 2
ff
f
II.[ff]
ff
Hei - - - - lig - tum. Seid um - - schlun - gen,
sf sf sf
Kuß der gan - zen Welt! Freu - de, schö - ner Göt - ter - fun - ken,
tum, dein Hei - - - - - - lig - tum. Seid um - - schlun - - - gen,
tre - ten dein Hei - - - - - lig - tum. Seid
ff
sf
f f
f f f
f f f
ff

703
a 2
a 2
in La/A
a 2
II. [f]
f
in Re/D
in Re/D
seid ___ um - - - schlun - gen
Toch - ter aus E - ly - si - um ___, Wir be - tre - ten feu - er - trun - ken,
seid um - - - schlun -
___ um - - - schlun - gen! Die - - - sen Kuß der
[ff]
f
f
f
sf

Q
707
a 2
a 2
a 2
Mil - - li - - o - - nen! Mil - - - li - o - - nen!
Himm - li - sche, dein Hei - lig - tum. Seid um - - schlun - gen
- - - gen, seid um - - schlun - gen
gan - - zen Welt! Freu - de, schö - ner Göt - ter - fun - ken,
Q
f f f f

711
a 2
a 2
a 2
in La/A
in Re/D
in Re/D
Die - - - sen Kuß, die - - - - - sen Kuß der
Mil - - li - - - o - - - nen! Die - - - sen Kuß der
Mil - - li - - - o - - - nen! Die - - - sen Kuß der
Toch - ter aus E - ly - si - um Wir be - tre - ten feu - er - trun - ken,
sf f f f
sf
sf
Vc. e B.

715
a 2
a 2
a 2
II. ff
II. [ff]
gan - - - zen Welt, der gan - - zen Welt
gan - - - zen, gan - - - zen Welt !
gan - - - zen Welt, der gan - zen
Himm - li - sche, dein Hei - - - - - lig - tum.
Seid
non ligato

720
a 2
in La/A
in Re/D
in Re/D
Freu - de, schö - ner Göt - ter - fun - ken, Toch - ter aus E - ly - si - um, Wir be - tre - ten,
Welt ! Seid um - schlun - gen Mil - li -
um - schlun - gen Mil - li - o - nen! Die - sen
sempre non ligato

725
a 2
a 2
a 2
II. [f] II. [f] II. f II. f II. [ff] II. [f] II. [f]
f f f f ff f f
Himm - li-sche, dein Hei - - - - - - - - - - lig-tum.
, der gan - zen Welt !
o - - nen ! Die - - - - sen Kuß der gan - zen Welt!
Kuß der gan - zen, gan - - - - - - zen Welt!
Vc. e B.
f f f f ff f f

730
R
a 2
pp
in La/A
in Re/D
in Re/D
p
Ah - nest du den Schöp - fer, Welt?
Ihr stürzt nie - der, Mil - li - o - nen?
R

738
p cresc.
a 2
cresc.
a 2
cresc.
cresc.
p cresc.
Such' ihn ü - berm Ster - nen-
cresc.
cresc.
Such' ihn ü - berm Ster - nen - zelt,
such' ihn ü - berm Ster - nen-
cresc.
Such' ihn ü - berm Ster - nen-
cresc.
Such' ihn ü - berm Ster - nen-
cresc.
cresc.
cresc.
cresc.

745
in La/A
in Re/D
in Re/D
II. p
zelt! Brü - der! Brü - der! ü - - berm Ster - - - - nen - zelt Muß
zelt! Brü - der! Brü - der! ü - - berm Ster - - - - nen - zelt Muß
zelt! Brü - der! Brü - der! ü - - berm Ster - - - - nen - zelt Muß
zelt! Brü - der! Brü - der! ü - - berm Ster - - - - nen - zelt Muß

754
a 2
a 2
[p]
più p
II. più p
pp
ppp
ein lie - ber Va - ter woh - nen, ein lie - ber Va - ter woh - - nen.
ein lie - ber Va - ter woh - nen, ein lie - ber Va - ter woh - - nen.
ein lie - ber Va - ter woh - nen, ein lie - ber Va - ter woh - - nen.
ein lie - ber Va - ter woh - nen, ein lie - ber Va - ter woh - - nen.

763
Allegro ma non tanto 𝅗𝅥 = 120
Fl. I II
Ob. I II
Clar. I II in La/A
Fag. I II
II. pp
Cor. in Re/D I II
III IV
Clno. I II in Re/D
Timp.
SOLI
Sop.
Alt.
Ten.
Toch - - - ter,
Bar.
Toch - - - ter,
Allegro ma non tanto 𝅗𝅥 = 120
Viol. I
II
Vle.
sempre pp
Vc. e B.

768
pp
pp
pp
Freu - - - de_, Toch - ter aus E - ly - si-um!
Freu - - - de_, Toch - ter aus E - ly - si-um!
Toch - ter aus E - ly - si-um!
Toch - ter aus E - ly - si-um!
sempre pp
sempre pp
pp

773
pp
in La/A
II. pp
I.
in Re/D
[pp]
in Re/D
Toch - - - ter_,
Toch - - - ter_,
sempre pp
sempre pp

778
I.
II.
pp
Toch - ter aus E - ly - si-um! Dei -
Toch - ter aus E - ly - si-um!
Toch - - ter _, Toch - ter aus E - ly - si-um!
Toch - - ter _, Toch - ter aus E - ly - si-um!
pp

783
in La/A
in Re/D
in Re/D
cresc. poco a poco
cresc.
- ne Zau-ber, deine Zau-ber bin - den wie - der, dei - ne Zau - ber bin - den wie - der, Was die Mo-de
Deine Zau-ber, deine Zau-ber bin - den wie - der, dei-ne Zau-ber, dei-ne Zau-ber bin - den wie - der,
Dei-ne Zau-ber, deine Zau-ber bin - den wie - der, bin - den, bin - den wie - der,
Dei-ne Zau-ber, dei-ne Zau-ber bin - den wie - der, dei - ne
pizz.
Vc.
B.

792
S
Fl. I II
Ob. I II
a 2
Clar. I II
a 2
Fag. I II
Cor. I II III IV
Clno. I II
Timp.
SOLI
Sop.
streng ge-teilt, Dei - ne Zau-ber, dei-ne Zau-ber bin - den _ wie - der _, Was die Mo-de streng
Alt.
bin - den, bin - den wie - der, Was _ die Mo-de streng
Ten.
dei-ne Zau-ber, dei-ne Zau-ber bin - den _ wie - der _, Was die Mo-de streng
Bar.
Zau - ber _ bin - den _ wie - der _, Was die Mo-de streng
CORO
Sop.
p cresc.
Deine Zau-ber, deine Zau-ber bin - den _ wie - der _, bin - den _ wie - der _,
Alt.
p cresc.
Deine Zau-ber, deine Zau-ber bin - den _ wie - der _, bin - den _ wie - der _,
Ten.
p cresc.
Deine Zau-ber, deine Zau-ber bin - den _ wie - der _, bin - den _ wie - der _,
Bass.
p cresc.
Deine Zau-ber, deine Zau-ber bin - den _ wie - der _, bin - den _ wie - der _,
Viol. I II
arco
Vle.
arco
Vc. e B.
arco

801
a 2
in La/A
in Re/D
in Re/D
p cresc.
ge - teilt.
Was die Mo - de streng ge - teilt.
Al - le
Vc.
B.

poco adagio
807
Menschen, al - le Menschen, al - le Menschen, al - le Menschen wer-den Brü-der, Wo dein sanf - - ter
Menschen, al - le Menschen, al - le Menschen, al - le Menschen wer-den Brü-der, Wo dein sanf - - ter
Menschen, al - le Menschen, al - le Menschen, al - le Menschen wer-den Brü-der, Wo dein sanf - - ter
Menschen, al - le Menschen, al - le Menschen, al - le Menschen wer-den Brü-der, Wo dein sanf - - ter
poco adagio
espressivo
p dolce
Vc. e B.

Tempo I
813
in La/A
in Re/D
in Re/D
a 2
p
cresc.
[p]
p cresc.
Flü - gel weilt.
Deine Zauber, deine Zauber bin - den
Flü - gel weilt.
Deine Zauber, deine Zauber bin - den
Flü - gel weilt.
Deine Zauber, deine Zauber bin - den
Flü - gel weilt.
Deine Zauber, deine Zauber bin - den
Tempo I

821
a 2
wie - der_, Was die Mo - de streng ge - teilt.
wie - der, Was die Mo - de streng ge - teilt.
wie - der_, Was die Mo - de streng ge - teilt.
wie - der, Was die Mo - de streng ge - teilt.
Vc.
B.
cresc.

827
in La/A
in Re/D
in Re/D
Al - le Men - schen, al - le,
Al - le Men - schen, al - le,
Al - le Men - schen, al - le,
Al - le Men - schen, al - le,
Al - le Men - schen, al - le Men - schen, al - le Men - schen, al - le
Al - le Men - schen, al - le Men - schen, al - le Men - schen, al - le
Al - le Men - schen, al - le Men - schen, al - le Men - schen, al - le
Al - le Men - schen, al - le Men - schen, al - le Men - schen, al - le
Vc. e B.

*) Regarding Chorus, cf. / Zum Chor, vgl. Critical Commentary.

838
in La/A
in Re/D
in Re/D
cresc.
Flü-gel weilt, dein sanf - - - - - ter Flü-gel _ weilt ____ .
cresc.
Flü-gel weilt, dein sanf - - - - - ter Flü-gel _ weilt ____ .
cresc.
- - - - - ter _ Flü-gel weilt, dein sanf - ter Flü - gel _ weilt ____ .
cresc.
— , dein sanf - - - - - - - ter Flü-gel weilt ____ .

843
poco Allegro, stringendo il tempo, sempre più Allegro
Fl. picc.
Fl. I II
Ob. I II
Clar. I II
Fag. I II
Cfg.
Cor. I II III IV
Clno. I II
Timp.
SOLI
Sop.
Alt.
Ten.
Bar.
CORO
Sop.
Alt.
Ten.
Bass.
poco Allegro, stringendo il tempo, sempre più Allegro
Viol. I II
Vle.
Vc. e B.
a 2
cresc.
pp

Presto 𝅗𝅥 = 132
851
Fl. picc.
Fl. I II
a 2
Ob. I II
Clar. I II in La/A
Fag. I II
Cfg.
Cor. I II in Re/D
III IV
Clno. I II in Re/D
Trb. I II
III
Timp.
Trgl.
Cin. Gr. Tamb.
CORO
Sop.
Alt.
Ten.
Bass.
Seid um-schlun-gen Mil-li - o-nen! Die-sen Kuß der gan-zen Welt!
Presto 𝅗𝅥 = 132
Viol. I
II
Vle.
Vc. e B.

859
a 2
a 2
a 2
a 2
sf f f f
der gan-zen Welt ! Brü - der!
der gan-zen Welt ! Brü - der!
der gan-zen Welt ! Brü - der!
der gan-zen Welt ! Brü - der!

865
a 2
in La/A
in Re/D
in Re/D
ü - berm Ster - nen - zelt Muß ein lie - ber Va - ter, ein lie - ber
ü - berm Ster - nen - zelt Muß ein lie - ber Va - ter, ein lie - ber
ü - berm Ster - nen - zelt Muß ein lie - ber Va - ter, ein lie - ber
ü - berm Ster - nen - zelt Muß ein lie - ber Va - ter, ein lie - ber

871
a 2
Va - ter wohn - - - - nen, ein lie - ber Va - ter wohn-nen.
Va - ter woh - - - - nen, ein lie - ber Va - ter woh-nen.
Va - ter woh - - - - nen, ein lie - ber Va - ter woh-nen.
Va - ter woh - - - - nen, ein lie - ber Va - ter woh-nen.

877
a 2
in La/A
in Re/D
in Re/D
Seid um-schlun-gen! seid um-schlun-gen! Die - sen Kuß der gan - zen Welt, der
Seid um-schlun-gen! seid um-schlun-gen! Die - sen Kuß der gan - zen Welt, der
Seid um-schlun-gen! seid um-schlun-gen! Die - sen Kuß der gan - zen Welt, der
Seid um-schlun-gen! seid um-schlun-gen! Die - sen Kuß der gan - zen Welt, der

884
T
a 2
gan - zen Welt, der gan - zen Welt! Die - sen Kuß der gan - zen Welt, der
gan - zen Welt, der gan - zen Welt! Die - sen Kuß der gan - zen Welt, der
gan - zen Welt, der gan - zen Welt! Die - sen Kuß der gan - zen Welt, der
gan - zen Welt, der gan - zen Welt! Die - sen Kuß der gan - zen Welt, der
T

892
in La/A
in Re/D
in Re/D
a 2
gan - zen Welt, der gan - zen, gan -
gan - zen Welt, der gan - zen, gan -
gan - zen Welt, der gan - zen, gan -
gan - zen Welt, der gan - zen, gan -

898
- - zen Welt, der gan - - - - - - - - - - - - - zen Welt!
- - zen Welt, der gan - - - - - - - - - - - - - zen Welt!
- - zen Welt, der gan - - - - - - - - - - - - - zen Welt!
- - zen Welt, der gan - - - - - - - - - - - - - zen Welt!

904
a 2
in La/A
a 2
in Re/D
in Re/D
Freu - de, Freu - de, schö - ner Göt - - - ter - fun - ken! schö - ner
Freu - de, Freu - de, schö - ner Göt - - - ter - fun - ken! schö - ner
Freu - de, Freu - de, schö - ner Göt - - - ter - fun - ken! schö - ner
Freu - de, Freu - de, schö - ner Göt - - - ter - fun - ken! schö - ner

910
a 2
a 2
a 2
Göt - - - - ter - fun - ken!
Toch -
Göt - - - - ter - fun - ken!
Toch -
Göt - - - - ter - fun - ken!
Toch -
Göt - - - - ter - fun - ken!
Toch -

Maestoso ♩ = 60
916
in La/A
in Re/D
in Re/D
a 2
- ter aus E - ly-si-um! Freu - de, schö - - ner Göt - ter-fun - ken! Göt - ter-
- ter aus E - ly-si-um! Freu - de, schö - - ner Göt - ter-fun - ken! Göt - ter-
- ter aus E - ly-si-um! Freu - de, schö - - ner Göt - ter-fun - ken! Göt - ter-
- ter aus E - ly-si-um! Freu - de, schö - - ner Göt - ter-fun - ken! Göt - ter-
Maestoso ♩ = 60
Vc.
B.

*) Cf. / Vgl. Critical Commentary.

926
a 2
in La/A
in Re/D
in Re/D
a 2
Vc. e B.
sf
f
sempre ff

933
sf
ff
a 2
6

BÄRENREITER CLASSICS

Franz Schubert

Sämtliche Kammermusik-Werke im Taschenbuch
The Complete Chamber Music in paperback

Band 1: Kammermusik unterschiedlicher Besetzung
Band 2: Sämtliche Streichquartette
Band 3: Kammermusik mit Klavier

Volume 1: Chamber Musik with Varied Instrumentation
Volume 2: Complete String Quartets
Volume 3: Chamber Music with Piano

BVK 1280

Bärenreiter

A 184 · 9901